About the a

Vyvyan Kinross is an experienced PR advisor who co-founded his own PR and marketing firm and grew it into the UK top 50. He now focuses on training and coaching PR professionals in a wide range of workplace skills both in the UK and abroad, including western and eastern Europe, the USA, Africa and the Middle East.

Vyvyan started his career as a journalist with IPC Business Press, specialising in Middle East trade, economics, health and transport issues. He travelled widely in the region as a reporter and feature writer, including to Saudi Arabia, Kuwait, Iraq, Syria and the West Bank. In 1981, he reported on the Iran Iraq war and, whilst at IPC Business Press, was nominated as feature writer of the year. He has a degree in Modern Arabic Studies from the University of Durham.

In 2011, he helped design new PR processes for the Government Municipalities of Abu Dhabi. Most recently, Vyvyan has authored content on effective communications and the written word for the UK's new PR Higher Apprenticeship scheme, designed to attract more school leavers and greater diversity of young people into the PR profession.

Vyvyan is a member of both the Public Relations Consultants Association (PRCA) and the Chartered Institute of Public Relations (CIPR).
He is married with two children and lives in West London.

THE CATERPILLAR FACTORY

KICK START YOUR CAREER IN THE PR BUSINESS

VYVYAN KINROSS

Matador
9 Priory Business Park,
Wistow Road, Kibworth Beauchamp,
Leicestershire. LE8 0RX
Tel: (+44) 116 279 2299
Fax: (+44) 116 279 2277
Email: books@troubador.co.uk
Web: www.troubador.co.uk/matador

ISBN 978 1780885 063

British Library Cataloguing in Publication Data.
A catalogue record for this book is available from the British Library.

Printed and bound in the UK by TJ International, Padstow, Cornwall
Typeset in 11pt Aldine401 BT Roman by Troubador Publishing Ltd, Leicester, UK

Matador is an imprint of Troubador Publishing Ltd

For S.J.K.

"*That the manufacture of consent is capable of great refinements no-one, I think, denies. The process by which public opinions arise is certainly no less intricate than it has appeared in these pages and the opportunities for manipulation open to anyone who understands the process are plain enough.*"

Walter Lippmann, Public Opinion, 1922

Preface

The public relations business is on the march. The UK PR industry alone turns over £7.5 billion each year, with about £2 billion accounted for by consultancies and the balance by in-house spending.* What's more, the industry's annual turnover is on an upwards trajectory and increasing numbers of young people in the UK and around the world are being attracted into the profession as a first-choice career.

This book will help all students of public relations, including existing practitioners, who want a practical introduction to PR consulting, its principal processes, how it is applied and the necessary skills required to succeed at it. The book is not academic in its approach, but more of a technical 'how to' book which assumes a basic understanding of PR and communications theory, its applied context, common language and standard references.

The book addresses especially students planning a career in PR, those new to the PR business and those working their way up agencies. PR professionals who are studying for industry qualifications may also find something here for them. The book, to some degree, also speaks to those needing to take responsibility for the PR and communications functions inside organisations, those commissioning consultancy but not sure how to buy it and entrepreneurs looking to set up their own PR businesses, either as freelancers or alongside others.

How is it different to all those other PR books out there? Firstly, the focus of the book is on PR skills, processes and the business of consulting, rather than the wider field of generic public relations. It therefore steers away from repeating content you can get from a broad spread of existing works either driven by an academic agenda or a specialist focus, for example, on social media or crisis management. Secondly, it does not attempt to cover every aspect of modern PR and communications practice from drawing board to boardroom,

*PR Census 2011, PR Week and the Public Relations Consultants Association (PRCA), Harris Interactive.

but is filtered through a personal view of the applied knowledge, structural approach and tools required to be more effective in the workplace. Therefore, it goes narrow and deep rather than wide and shallow.

The idea behind the book is to set out the chain that links the separate stages of the PR consultancy process, giving an end-to-end view of how each part and the whole work together. The Caterpillar Factory therefore spans the nuts and bolts of the business, taking as its starting point the nature of consulting itself. How do you define the contract between consultant and client and what is the fundamental nature of the PR consultant's contribution and therefore value to an organisation? The book explains the basic PR consultancy business model to show how profitable work is organised and people motivated and managed. It also sets out how PR consultants typically approach and generate new business opportunities by setting up a sales pipeline and offers a best practice template to help craft proposals to win business, both critical building blocks of the consultancy process.

A particular focus of the book is on the role of the media in PR and the practice of media relations, most especially the management and exploitation of news and the role of features in generating deeper and more lasting insight and media coverage for clients. The book also unlocks some of the thinking behind developing effective spokespeople and sets out the route to planning and pulling off successful media interviews.

Other subjects that are links in the chain include a proven structure and methodology to apply to PR launches, a traditionally high-risk area for PR consultants. The book also provides an overview of the main genres of PR writing and gives some basic rules and ideas to help construct consistency and style across written outputs, a prerequisite of effective communications.

The Caterpillar Factory offers a general insight into the role and working life of the typical caterpillar in today's agency world, giving a feel for a range of roles. It also throws some light on a select few of the most illustrious though sometimes neglected caterpillars of all, among them the founding fathers of modern public relations, 'engineers of consent' such as Edward Bernays, Ivy Ledbetter Lee and Carl Byoir.

Throughout, its approach is pragmatic rather than prescriptive, centred on first-hand, front-line experience of the PR consultancy business. What's more it is made practical and interactive through the inclusion of exercises and suggestions to test the reader's knowledge and skills in some subject areas; these are then supported with answers towards the back of the book. Whilst the book has been constructed to be accessed in a linear fashion, the reader should feel free to approach any one of the links in the PR chain independently and at will.

Perhaps most tellingly, much of the content of The Caterpillar Factory has already been evaluated by hundreds of PR students and professionals in face-to-face and online training sessions across the UK and abroad. That is because it brings together and amplifies for the first time a number of successful training programmes developed over the last decade and deployed in the marketplace with a diverse range of consultancy and in-house teams and individuals.

Above all, this book is for would-be caterpillars who want a front-line insight into the PR life and whether it might be for them.

"The caterpillar does all the work but the butterfly gets all the publicity."
American comedian George Carlin, 1937-2008

Contents

Public Relations and Consulting

Introduction; topography of consultancy; competition as a driver; attributes of PR consultants; the debate over PR consultancy; the digital dimension.

Introduction

One of my recurring observations of people is just how good, and keen, some are at promoting themselves and just how reluctant and inexpert are some others. What's more, the appetite for promotion, or self-promotion, too often seems to operate in inverse proportion to the quality of the commodity on offer.

This is an observation primarily based in the world of work, but not exclusively so. Some of us seem born for the spotlight whilst others are prepared to toil away in the engine room, unsung but making our contribution nonetheless. In today's celebrity culture it is those who shout loudest who get the attention, those who actively build their brand who get the signature clothing line or reality TV show.

Like everything else, the notion of shouting loudly has long since become professionalised; the age of the enthusiastic amateur has passed. Added to which, doing the heavy lifting whilst stuck in the background doesn't seem like the smart business move these days; if people can't 'see' you, why should they care about you? Thus, we now have experts who tell us that our messages have to achieve cut-through, that we have to be heard above the noise, that we must fight for share of voice, be top of mind and 'always on'. Shouting loudly even has its own language, developed, colonised and monetised exclusively by insiders.

Let me confess right now to being one of those insiders. I have often sat across a meeting room table from clients and told them in so many words: "We should be generating more heat around this issue, we have a compelling story that the market needs to hear. The problem is we aren't getting our message across where it really matters." This, and conversations like it, are part of the lexicon and vernacular of the public relations practitioner.

To paraphrase George Carlin, the PR practitioner is a professional caterpillar, dedicated to releasing beautiful butterflies which dazzle with their brilliance, make a splash, get talked about and win prizes. It is the choice of the caterpillar to engineer the butterfly's success covertly from somewhere offstage in the wings, hidden from public gaze. It is the destiny of the caterpillar to be the kingmaker, rather than the king.

These days, some PR practitioners transcend the caterpillar life cycle and reincarnate themselves as butterflies, but they remain rare exceptions to the general rule; the publicist Max Clifford and Tony Blair's ubiquitous former head of communications Alastair Campbell come to mind – and even then they remain caterpillars by temperament and training.

The fact is that PR practitioners now outnumber journalists in the UK. In 2008, the graphs crossed for the first time at 47,800 and 45,000 respectively; *. Now the number of jobs generated by the UK PR sector has risen even further to 61,000, according to the 2011 PR Week/PRCA Census.

So who are PR practitioners exactly and should they be a worry? Opinions vary and it is true that there is a wide spectrum that accommodates both the simple publicist and the sophisticated head of corporate communications working alongside senior management in a FTSE 100 company. It is fair, though, to characterise both extremes in their own way as professional communicators whose job is to help their clients work out what they have to say and then help them say it, get heard and seen in the right places and evoke the desired attitudinal or behavioural response from their chosen audience.

Just as opinions vary as to the precise role of the PR practitioner, opinion is divided as to what precise purpose public relations serves. In 1990, the American author Stuart Ewen went to meet the founder of modern public relations practice, Edward L Bernays, at his home in Cambridge Massachusetts; Bernays was then nearly a centenarian. After a five hour interview with the legendary master manipulator, Ewen wrote: "Ideally, the job of public relations is not simply one of disseminating favourable images and impressions for a client. For Bernays and, as I would learn for many others in the field, the goal was far more

---

Flat Earth News, Nick Davies, Chatto & Windus, 2008.

ambitious than that. Public relations was about fashioning and projecting credible renditions of reality itself."*

Manipulation of the public mood and shaping of mass opinion, often for crudely self-interested motives, is an accusation that PR as a profession has regularly had to confront since it surfaced over a century ago. Though it is wired into the PR manifesto that no practitioner should put a client's interests before those of society as a whole, this central proposition is sometimes overlooked by both sides of the PR divide, both in principle and practice.

The architect of the world's largest PR consultancy, Harold Burson, defines public relations as an applied social science that influences behaviour and policy and, when communicated effectively, motivates an individual or group to a specific course of action, by creating, changing or reinforcing opinions or attitudes.** His caveat is that public relations should never be practised at the expense of the public interest, which he claims ultimately coincides with the client interest.

The fact is that PR itself, ironically, still gets a poor press and is mundanely bracketed as a dark art or dismissed as spin rather than being assessed in a more measured way, for example, as one defined business process amongst a number of complementary and interlocking processes. Somewhere between this simplistic, overly negative interpretation and the demand for modern, professionalised communications a more sophisticated accommodation and consensus on the ethical dimension of PR is still being arrived at.

Topography of consultancy

Whether it happens in-house or in agencies, public relations practice implies professional expertise in the wider world of corporate communications and reputation management. Its genesis is scientific, to be found in the associated fields of systems theory, communications modelling, propaganda, persuasion and power/interest matrices. The earliest PR practitioners, men like Edward Bernays and Ivy Lee (see Chapter Twelve, Caterpillars of Wisdom), used methodologies and tools derived from Freudian psychological principles, social science and propaganda to persuade and manipulate the public into a desired

---

*'PR! A Social History Of Spin', Stuart Ewen, Basic Books 1996
**www.haroldburson.com

response. They also imported tools and techniques from journalistic practice and adapted them to suit their own needs, principally to access and exploit the news agenda. The development of the news release in 1906 is a classic example of this adaptive approach.

The consultancy process, whether temporary or permanent, internal or external, enables buyers or users to tap into this professional expertise. Individuals and businesses hire PR consultants for their ability to fulfill three key functions: to *analyse* the prevailing commercial or organisational environment and evaluate in a rigorous way any resulting business intelligence; to *advise* senior management on a timely course of action to further their organisation's interests; and third to *execute* action-based communications programmes aimed at altering perceptions and changing audience behaviours. It is just as well to know right at the start what consulting means as this is sometimes misunderstood. Your ability to grasp and manipulate these three core functions is instrumental in deciding whether you are, or aspire to be, a consultant.

One thing is for sure. People will not pay a high price to hire a PR consultant or advisor just to share a few uncertainties. When you pay for consultancy you are buying a mix of *time and expertise* applied to your individual business situation and consequent communications challenge. You are not expecting an off-the-peg solution first designed for a widget manufacuter down the road, nor are you expecting hedged advice; the client interest is to buy the original, the definitive. Thus it pays from the start to know what is expected from the role and your representation of it.

Wikipedia, the constant companion of journalists and PRs, defines a consultant (from Latin: *consultare* "to discuss") as a professional who provides professional or expert advice in a particular area such as security (electronic or physical), management, accountancy, law (tax law, in particular), human resources, marketing (and public relations), finance, engineering, or any of many other specialised fields.

The consulting guru Peter Block, author of *'Flawless Consulting: A Guide To Getting Your Expertise Used'* identifies a consultant as 'someone who has influence over an individual, group, or organisation, but who has no direct authority to implement changes.' He contrasts this with a *surrogate manager* who is a person who 'acts on behalf of, or in place of, a manager.' The key difference is that a consultant never makes decisions for the individual or group, whereas a surrogate manager does make decisions.

A consultant therefore is usually an expert or a professional in a specific field and has a wide knowledge of the subject matter. Overall the impact of a consultant is that clients have access to deeper levels of expertise than would be feasible for them to retain in-house, and may purchase only as much service from the outside consultant as desired.

Thus planning and managing the intervention of a PR consultancy creates in itself a certain level of expectation and associated pressure for the consultant, or consultancy. That is, in short, that the intervention will result in value being added through the agreed analysis and subsequent inputs and outputs. To be justified, consultancy therefore must add measurable value either to an organisation's performance or processes, or both. When competently executed, PR consultancy offers a careful balance between analysis, strategic advice and tactical implementation. Consultants who, by virtue of their own limitations, cannot think strategically tend to experience arrested career development and get bracketed merely as implementers, thus restricting their value to organisations and limiting their own rise through the profession.

In public relations, it is the methodology employed to articulate or measure added value, sometimes referred to as Return on Investment (ROI), which is at the heart of the argument about the quantifiable contribution the discipline makes to an organisation's bottom line. This argument is complex, somewhat vexed and dynamic, and furthermore lies at the root of the past failure of PR to make a more rapid and wholesale advance into the boardroom.

However, whilst the search for the ultimate, definitive answer to the value question may consume the upper management layers of the profession, there can be no doubt that PR, through its various permutations of outputs, out-takes and outcomes (see Chapter Four, Writing Winning PR Proposals) provides the kind of tangible value that can't be replicated in other promotional disciplines.

Public relations consulting is just one of a number of areas where consultancy is used to add value to businesses. Perhaps the best known of these is management consultancy, which is the longest established form of consultancy in the business sphere. The first management consultancy firm, Arthur D Little, was founded as early as 1886; its PR equivalent, Parker & Lee was founded in 1905, with the better known and longer lived Ivy Lee & Associates opening for business as late as 1919.

We all tend to be familiar with the highest profile global management consultancy brands, such as McKinseys, the Boston Consulting Group or Bain & Company, but much less so with the long established global public relations brands like Edelman or Hill & Knowlton. This relative lack of visibility is partly about scale and partly about perceptions of added value, but it also reflects the fact that the work of the PR practitioner is simply lower profile and less well understood by both consumers and business than some other disciplines.

Over and above management consultants, the most commonly found consultants in commerce are: strategy consultants working on the development of and improvements to organisational strategy alongside senior management in many industries; human resources (HR) consultants who provide expertise around employment practice and people management; or Internet consultants who are specialists in business use of the internet and keep themselves up to date with new and changed capabilities offered by the web.

Other consultants in the business 'family' might include process consultants, who are specialists in the design or improvement of operational processes and can be specific to the industry or sector, for example, through the application of business process re-engineering (BPR) techniques and tools; performance consultants, who focus on the execution of an intuitive or overall performance of the client; or information technology consultants in many disciplines such as computer hardware, software engineering or networks.

Competition as a driver

A concept that is intrinsic to the idea behind buying or selling public relations consultancy, or indeed most consultancy, is the notion of the competitive pitch. PR consultants generally do not expect to be handed out work to do by clients; they have to compete against other PR consultants to win business. The process involves responding to a written brief with a detailed proposal, a subsequent pitch or presentation where ideas can be showcased and the awarding of a contract to the consultancy which establishes a framework within which the work will be delivered.

Part of the work of the consultant, therefore, is an understanding of the new business process and mastery of the techniques required to compete successfully against others. This is addressed in more detail in this book in Chapters Three and Four.

It is therefore part of the consultancy landscape to always be somewhere on the competitive arc, either creating new business opportunities, responding to briefs, pitching for work or delivering work already booked. Because of the nature of business and the way it favours specialists over generalists, many PR consultancies will choose to specialise, for example in technology or professional services, because it increases their chances of winning new business. The biggest agencies will have specialist divisions or subsidiaries which offer services grouped around vertical sector niches or by skill sets, for example social & digital media.

Where people are trying to make career decisions about PR, and how and where to specialise, you could argue that the choice as to whether to practise PR in-house (inside an organisation) or externally, in a consultancy, is perhaps the most fundamental. Each has their advantages and disadvantages, but the inability or lack of desire to participate in the new busines cycle would arguably be the single greatest determinant in this context.

Attributes of PR consultants

It is almost axiomatic that organisations do not hire PR consultancies to do things that they could do themselves. It would be curious if they did. In fact, organisations hire PR consultancies just because of their ability to do things that cannot be realised in-house for one reason or another. In some cases, this might be strategic thinking around the positioning of a brand or product, in others perhaps the development and roll-out of a specific information campaign to promote a new initiative.

In any event, PR consultants are expected to bring certain recurring attributes to the table. One of these is *creativity*. More often than not, PR consultancy is used for its ability to come up with a creative solution to a communications challenge. It might be a campaign theme, a stunt, a brand idea, a superlative media pitch or the use of a particular champion to provide media traction for a new product. Without creative chutzpah, PR consultancy can look a little threadbare; therefore, it especially suits people who can conceptualise and develop strong ideas and turn them into hard campaign currency.

Likewise, clients will buy consultancy because of its ability to open up the doors to a series of *networks*. The most successful PR consultants are usually highly networked people, and these networks can extend deep into industry and media sectors, across borders into different geographies, and upwards into the corridors of the political, establishment, industrial and arts powerbase. In the battle to become visible and relevant, the ability to create and leverage networks can be the deciding factor between success or failure in carving out a market presence.

Perhaps most of all though, consultancies can make things happen by doing, based on their intimate and deep understanding of audiences, communications methodologies, tools and techniques. They have the resources, the teams, the expertise and the focus to develop *action-based* communications programmes which deliver outcomes and change behaviours in ways that cannot be replicated elsewhere across the sales, marketing and promotional spectrum. Therein, perhaps, lies PR's real differentiator from other marketing related disciplines.

As one might expect, it is hard to generalise about the qualities that most lend themselves to successful PR people. This is partly because it is a profession that attracts individualists, often with strong self-belief and egos to match, who believe that they can make a difference by doing things their way.

Thus on one level it attracts entrepreneurs, showmen and alchemists, in the tradition of P.T. Barnum and Ivy Lee. At the same time, though, PR is increasingly a profession of first-choice for many graduates, post-graduates and school leavers who are looking for a more conventional career path through the ranks of multinationals and large public sector organisations and charities, all of whom increasingly deploy sophisticated information and public relations campaigning as part of their marketing and promotional stance. They see PR as a young, dynamic profession which is riding the wave of change that spans organisational, business and social hierarchies; it is therefore a broad church which can accommodate a diverse congregation.

PR undoubtedly has room for specialists and generalists, artists and artisans, the youthful and the more mature. Through this diversity, it is possible to discern some common threads that bind PR people together. To be successful, it helps to have a feel for the cultural and commercial zeitgeist, a general curiosity, a love of the communications process and a mastery of the tools of verbal and written expression. If you are highly articulate, write well and have a fascination for the fundamentals of dialogue, you are primed for a successful career entry.

Likewise, if you are gripped by the news agenda – headlines, feature stories and pictures – and get a massive lift from seeing your copy appear in a newspaper or break on Twitter, it is a strong sign that PR might be for you. Conversely, if you are someone made anxious and perplexed by the imperfections of the sometimes shaky science behind media relations, you could be headed for early disillusionment.

It is also extremely helpful to have a fundamental curiosity about organisations and how they work. Some of the best PRs are those who, as it were, like to get their heads under the car bonnet and take the engine apart before putting it together again. It is actually very hard to deal on an equal footing with clients, say in a front-line business context, when you have only a very shallow understanding of how business in general really works, so a fascination for and knowledge of the mechanics and *dynamics of commerce* is very helpful. Some would go further and argue that the next generation of PR practitioners will need MBAs rather than MAs.

It is something of a cliché, but the PR profession is a people business and it therefore especially suits extroverts and those who fundamentally like the process of interaction with colleagues, clients, the media, business and the consumer. At best, PR consultancy is a full-on, full-time, high energy ride that takes few prisoners and yet can yield a high level of engagement, intellectual satisfaction and financial reward.

The debate over PR consultancy

It is significant that some PR consultancies or agencies remain reluctant to identify themselves entirely with the term 'public relations', as they perceive a potential downside or limitation through the association. Some of these agencies prefer to ally themselves more closely with the wider practice of corporate communications, perceptions management or even old-style publicity.

According to Paul Holmes, author of the Holmes Report, clients not intimately involved with the public relations industry may be surprised to learn that there is no consensus answer to the question of what precisely PR consultancy is, even among those who own and manage firms that call themselves public relations agencies.*

'Even those firms that continue to self-identify with the industry by making the term public relations part of their name will occasionally assure prospective clients that "we are not just a public relations agency" or that "what we do goes beyond traditional public relations," he says.

Traditional public relations consultancy is built around a model that has been in place for a number of years now. It has evolved and gained traction by adapting to the changing communications environment and by the increased sophistication of its approach to opening up and maintaining a dialogue with all kinds of stakeholders and audiences.

---

* Paul Holmes: the Holmes Report, 2012

The passage of this relatively modern discipline through the decades since the 1920s has been marked by its internal codification, formalisation and representation through professional bodies in the UK such as the Chartered Institute of Public Relations (www.cipr.co.uk) and the Public Relations Consultants Association (www.praca.org.uk).

It is worth noting that there was a time when the craft skills of PR were primarily journalistic, and transferred to professionals in a largely haphazard way by individual practitioners whose approach was to make sure that newcomers simply learned on the job, by first watching and then doing. Over time, though, this random and opportunistic approach has been overtaken by something altogether more systematic. Indeed, in the last 30 years, there has been a persistent process to codify the applied practice of public relations, with a new emphasis on continuing professional development (CPD), skills training programmes and the establishment of a system of professional qualifications. This has been supported by the spread of university and college degrees enabling full-time students to gain academic PR and media related qualifications (see Chapter Eleven: The Caterpillar Life).

The PR landscape is, however, very dynamic and always evolving. The social media revolution is just the latest in a line of game changers for PR consultants to accommodate in their strategic mindset and practical toolkit. In former years, it has been niche areas such as issues management, public affairs, crisis planning and management, investor relations and corporate social responsibility (CSR) that professionals have had to adopt and colonise as discrete areas for the development of service provision.

The digital dimension

However, the rapid spread of digital communications and social media in the last few years may to some extent be seen to be altering the traditional model and process of public relations practice. The arrival of real-time communications tools and establishment of something much closer to a dialogue of equals between brands and consumers is creating the room for a genuine paradigm shift.

The symmetrical communications model drawn up by the respected academics Grunig & Hunt, in which two-way communication between sender and receiver moves in perfect balance accommodating feedback and changing views as it goes, has traditionally been regarded as a kind of utopian ideal.

However, social media tools such as Twitter and Facebook have started to move this model onto the radar screen as a new reality for many businesses and consumer brands, which are increasingly deploying social media and digital communications to drive their stakeholder relationships.

What's more, the explosion in two-way digital communications and social media has meant that the 'pull' business model pioneered by the first movers of the Internet age, has now gained wider purchase, beginning to replace the old 'push' tools and techniques of industrial age marketing, changing the consumer landscape for ever.

"Helping buyers to buy, rather than sellers to sell, is the wave of the future. Right Side Up marketing – marketing for and on behalf of the consumer – is emerging to take its rightful place as the centre of marketing gravity," says Alan Mitchell in his ground-breaking book 'Right Side Up'.*

No single organisation exemplifies the potency and ubiquity of the social networking concept more than Facebook. "Facebook now sits squarely at the centre of a fundamental realignment of capitalism... marketing cannot be about companies shoving advertising in people's faces, not because it's wrong but because it doesn't work anymore," says David Kirkpatrick in 'The Facebook Effect'. **

This switch is revolutionising the way in which goods, services and ideas are marketed and promoted, requiring traditional relationships between organisations and their stakeholders to be rethought and recast. PR and communications consulting is directly concerned with shaping the subsequent conversation between buyers and sellers, producers and consumers, media and viewers and is thus at a crossroads in its own development and that of the very commercial process itself.

The continuing need to master this switch from analogue to digital communications, and to take leadership in its deployment and application to further client interests, is a prime reason why public relations is following a growth trajectory. Though this is a compelling reason, it is just one among many putting PR and communications closer to the centre of business and thus explains only in part why the lights of the caterpillar factory continue to burn long into the night.

---

*Right Side Up, Building Brands in the Age of the Organized Consumer', Alan Mitchell, Harper Collins Business, 2002.
**The Facebook Effect: The Inside Story of the company that is connecting the world, David Kirkpatrick, Simon & Schuster, 2010.

CHAPTER TWO

The Consultancy Business Model

Welcome to the bottom line; the role and importance of budgeting; getting to grips with management accounts; calculating capacity; setting fee rates; costing deliverables; monitoring budgets and PR programmes; the six rules of successful account management; using numbers to motivate the team; exercises.

Most consultants, and PR consultants are no exception, really sell just two things – time and expertise. Management, process and HR consultants, alongside lawyers and accountants, are some of the professionals who over the years have become extremely adept at charging in this way for their services. PR consultants occupy the same territory, although often without the same confidence or rigour.

But, however good you are at your job as a PR professional, you cannot hope to stay in business unless you can apply at least a basic consultancy business model, or at least your interpretation of it. That means making a return on your work, generally expressed as profit.

To do that, you must receive adequate reward for your work. This requires putting a price on your time and expertise which delivers a profit and *which the market will bear*. Above all, it must be a price that yields your organisation a level of return that will enable it to make capital investments, for example in new equipment, to market itself, reward and incentivise key people and provide a return to the owners, usually a combination of internal and external shareholders.

As if those weren't enough reasons, the code of conduct set out by the Chartered Institute of Public Relations (CIPR) isolates this aspect of the PR consulting role as a core competence, 'ensuring that services provided are costed and accounted for in a manner that conforms to accepted business practice and ethics'.

Harold Burson, regarded by some as the 20th century's most influential PR person, believes that public relations practitioners underprice their services. "It has been that way since I entered the profession six decades ago; for as long as I can remember, public relations practitioners have boasted that PR is the least costly way of reaching target audiences," he told delegates to the Public Relations World Congress in Dubai, in March 2012.

The typical profit margin in the PR business – the figure that is left over after deducting all operating expenses and depreciating capital equipment – reaches 20% or more in some cases. In tougher times, that figure slips to around 10% or less. A general truth probably sets the margin somewhere in between for most agencies, with distinct variations depending on sector or size of outfit; in 2011, for example, the top 150 UK PR consultancies had an average profit margin of 14.2%, according to industry magazine *PR Week*.

It is generally accepted that a profit margin below 10% leaves little wiggle room to accumulate vital cash without taking a punitive line with shareholders and suppliers – not good for business in the long run. The point here is that profit, and the cash that goes with it, provides the oil that greases the wheels of the business. Without it, the engine grinds to a halt. Thus everyone in the business has a responsibility to ensure they make a contribution to profit where they can. In this scenario, saving on costs can be as important as generating revenues. They both make a difference to the bottom line.

But for those at the fee-generating and management end of the business – associate directors, account directors, account managers and executives – contribution to profitability is one of the key performance indicators (KPIs) for doing a proper job. Whatever the sector, bonuses and jobs themselves depend on making a contribution to profit. Often the tools to manage the processes that generate profit are in place. Most businesses will claim they are. But often they are not, or only partially.

And sometimes, even when they are, no one takes the time to really explain how they work or they simply aren't used as effective management tools. It is important, therefore, to demystify the basic financial equations and processes that underpin the business of PR consultancy and unlock the potential of those who are to be held accountable as managers or executives for the first time. Whatever the processes in place in your own organisation, the general principles outlined here can be applied to benefit you and your team, and thus the organisation itself. More than anything, this is about developing plain business sense.

EXERCISE: Find out what your organisation's profit margin has been for the last three financial years. How do they compare against each other? Is there a trend?

The role and importance of budgeting

For many people, the word 'budget' still wants to make them run a mile. But rather than being intrinsically threatening, budgets are actually the principal compass that guides an organisation or department towards meeting its planned objectives. Budgets are there to help rather than hinder, to motivate and not inhibit. By definition, a budget is a plan for future activities, usually describing a business in financial terms.

As someone who may be new to PR consultancy, you might not have seen your organisation's budget. If not, ask the finance director to show you. It shouldn't be a secret. Budgeting is as useful for small organisations as it is for large ones, and a budget cycle should always be in place. However, it is axiomatic that all budgets are only as good as the people who prepare them. They also take time and generate paperwork.

It is more likely that you will already have a departmental or team budget to work towards. This shows you your departmental and personal responsibilities and targets, and creates a wider framework in which the whole company can work together as a team chasing the same end game. Budgets make you look ahead and anticipate – one of the secrets of successful management – and understanding them thoroughly delivers the knowledge and power to change the course of the business before it is too late.

The Six Main Aims Of Budgeting*

- *PLANNING*: to aid the planning of an organisation in a systematic and logical manner that adheres to the long-term business strategy

---

Managing Budgets', Stephen Brookson, Dorling Kindersley, 2001.

14

- *CO-ORDINATION*: to help co-ordinate the activities of the various parts of the organisation and ensure they are consistent
- *COMMUNICATION*: to communicate more easily the objectives, opportunities and plans of the business to the various team managers
- *MOTIVATION*: to provide motivation for managers to try to achieve the organisational and individual goals;
- *CONTROL*: to help control activities by measuring progress against the original plan, adjusting where necessary
- *EVALUATION*: to provide a framework for evaluating the performance of managers in meeting individual and departmental targets

Getting to grips with management accounts

This chapter is not designed to turn PRs into accountants, but rather to support them to understand the business they are in and thus become more effective consultants and better managers in the process. So the ability to read and understand management accounts is important if you are to see your own team's targets and performance in the context of the company as a whole. Getting your head around management accounts is all part of managing more effectively. Statistics show just how important this is. Monitoring what is happening to the revenue and cost streams within a company has the greatest impact on the probability of survival, when measured as a qualitative variable.*

All organisations of a certain size, consultancies or not, will produce management accounts on a monthly basis, usually just beyond the end of each calendar month. These accounts provide the levers you need to control the performance and direction of the business against budget. They allow you to change course while you have time to miss the iceberg. These accounts, expressed in columns of figures, will be produced on a spreadsheet and summarise the performance of the whole company in three distinct ways.

- They will give an absolute record of whether the company has made a profit or loss in that given month, and will break down this overall figure into a number of separate categories. Remember that, in accounting terms, a loss is always expressed through a figure contained in brackets, as in (£55.00) =

Surviving and Prospering In The Small Firms Sector, Graham Hall, Routledge, 1995.

a fifty pound loss. The appearance of brackets means 'less than'.

- The figures will also give a comparative measurement to show monthly performance against budget, with an additional column that identifies the variance between each category. By analysing these figures closely, a manager is able to see where the company has overspent or underspent, or performed better or worse on fees than predicted.

- Management accounts will also normally show how the company is performing against its budget set at the start of the financial year. This figure will be expressed through the measure of performance YTD, or Year To Date. It is an important figure for managers, because it allows corrective action to be taken at a point when it can still influence outcomes, rather than when it is already too late.

Accompanying the management accounts will usually be a cash flow statement that provides a record of how much money has come in or gone out during the course of the month. Without cash in the bank, a company's ability to function is extremely curtailed. In this respect, accounts that show a paper profit but no cash in the bank are flashing amber.

How would you respond if your boss told you he could not pay your salary at the end of the month because the bank account was empty? Hence the old adage: *'Revenue is vanity, profit is sanity, cash is king.'*

Calculating capacity

We've already seen that professional organisations make money by selling time and expertise. Some may sell proprietory products too, such as surveys or reports, but for the purposes of this chapter we shall stick with the primary two commodities. Senior management planners and finance directors will work out the revenue base of the company using a fairly simple formula to calculate the maximum revenue potential of the company as a whole. We'll call this the *total earnings capacity,* or TEC, being the maximum revenue a firm can generate from its human capital at any one time. Let's look at two examples of this.

EXAMPLE ONE

An account executive (AE) is charged out by the company at £250 per day, or

£36 per hour when rounded up. What is the maximum this person could generate in fees for the consultancy in one year? Consider:

- The AE is billable @ a maximum of 7 hours a day @ £36.00 = £250.00
- Total billable days per year: =231 days
  -From 365 days per year, deduct 104 for weekends
  -For annual leave, deduct 20 working days
  -For public holidays, deduct 7 working days
  -For annual sickness, deduct 3 working days

- **TEC calculation for Account Executive @ £250.00 x 231 days = £57,750.00**

EXAMPLE TWO

To calculate the earnings capacity of the company as a whole, an extrapolation of this equation is made across all employees, at all levels. This calculation is much more difficult to make, but it is critical for consultancies to try and at least establish what they could be earning at full capacity. Consider this non-mathematical formula as an illustration:

- Some employees, for example support staff, do not have any billable time (A):
- Fee earning staff are billing at different rates (B):
- Not all fee earners have the same amounts of billable time, for example directors who must allocate up to 25% of time to management (C)
- Resources are variable. People come and go, so the numbers follow them. This means the total TEC can vary from month to month or quarter to quarter (X).

- **TEC calculation for company as a whole : (X) = B + C – A**

Setting fee rates

It may be that you have your own definition of success. In the not-for-profit sector, for example, one might measure success by outcomes in terms of amounts of aid distributed, multiplied by the total numbers of recipients as a function of the cost of distribution. In the public sector, or in-house, other ways will be used to place an equivalent value on your time and level of outputs.

However, if you are a professional consultancy operating in a commercial environment, you cannot survive and prosper unless you are paid a rate for the job which does three distinct things:

- *Covers employees' salaries and National Insurance contributions*
- *Covers all fixed and variable costs*
- *Generates sufficient profit for reinvestment & distribution.*

Many professional businesses that sell time and expertise express this relationship through a standard formula of :

Target revenue (100%) = ALL salaries (33%) + costs (33%) + profits (33%).

They know that by aiming for a 33% profit margin, they are giving themselves a good chance of making a reasonable return, in the knowledge that salaries and costs are almost bound to come in higher than they have budgeted and revenues may well be lower. Hence, fee rates are most often calculated as a function of these three elements combined with total earnings capacity. The fee rates, applied to different levels of the agency staff, underpin all costings, whether for retainer or project based work, although some projects may carry a premium rate to incentivise clients to take up the offer of a retainer.

If the rates are too low, the business will be setting itself up to fail. However, all rates have to be in balance with what the market will bear – too high and you can price yourself out of a job, too low and your work will not be highly enough valued. Let's look at an *illustrative* agency fee rate structure (x7 hour day):

FIGURE I: FEE RATE CALCULATOR

POSITION	HOURLY RATE	DAILY RATE
Principal/Director (CP)	£143.00	£1,000.00

POSITION (continued...)	HOURLY RATE (continued...)	DAILY RATE (continued...)
Acct Director (AD)	£114.00	£800.00
Acct Manager (AM)	£71.00	£500.00
Acct Executive (AE)	£40.00	£280.00
Acct Administrator (AA)	£21.00	£150.00

Rates can vary, according to whether you work for a small, medium or large consultancy, or if you are a freelance with lower overheads. As a general rule, fee earning staff are expected to handle business three times higher than their salary in order to cover their share of overheads and make a contribution to profit.

It is worth making the point that some agencies, rather than calculating separate fee rates at different levels of the business, will take another route with the same goal. They will do one calculation of all fee rates for everyone in the business and then charge an *aggregated rate* for all the work the consultancy does for clients. This aggregated rate, which is an average of all levels, covers the costs of everyone, from seniors to juniors, and makes charging and costing comparatively much easier.

However, the issue with an aggregated rate is that it becomes more difficult to charge out senior people in the consultancy at their true earning power when they implement high value work, such as media training or communication audits. Clients, too, can sometimes question the notion of paying one rate for a job that doesn't necessarily always require a perfect balance of skills and levels.

Costing deliverables

We have already looked at how critical it is to set fee rates at a level which will balance the level of profit required by the business with what the market will bear. This is because no business, unless it is in a monopoly position, will be disconnected from the wider market within which it operates.

In the PR business, part of ensuring you get this equation right is the ability to place a cost, as accurately as possible, on the time and level of expertise required to produce a particular output, or 'deliverable'. Managers responsible for the salaries and performance of teams and even departments, will be asked to make judgements about the time required to complete tasks, whether one-off items such as a news release or an entire proposal with a serious price tag attached. In either case, it is in your interests to make these 'best guesses' as close as you can to reality. Why? Because you are likely to be held to them by clients who don't like nasty surprises and a bill that is double what they expected, or internally by senior managers and a finance director who are between them trying to resource and plan around the projected fee levels of your team, among a number of other profit centres.

Your organisation is already likely to have some form of calculator on which you can cost proposals by deliverable, but in any case consider the following illustrative guideline costs:

FIGURE 2: DELIVERABLES CALCULATOR

ITEM	TIME		TOTAL COST
News Release	1 day AE:	£280.00	£350.00
	1 hour AM	£71.00	
Case study/Feature	2 days AE	£560.00	£810.00
	0.5 day AM	£250.00	
Press Pack	3 days AE	£840.00	£1454.00
	1 day AM	£500.00	
	1 hour AD	£114.00	
Press Briefing	1 day AE	£280.00	£530.00
	½ day AM	£250.00	

Press Office (pcm)	2 days AE	£560.00	£1760.00
	1 day AM	£500.00	
	½ day AD	£400.00	
	2 days Admin	£300.00	
Speech	1 day AM	£500.00	£1330.00
	½ day AD	£400.00	
	1 day AE	£280.00	
	1 day Admin	£150.00	

EXERCISE: Cost out the provision of one year's press office, 12 news releases, two speeches, three case studies, one feature. What figure do you reach?

Monitoring budgets and PR programmes

Once the company has set and agreed its budget, the projected revenues need to be achieved and expenditure must not be exceeded. Your department or team's performance is integral to this, so you need a system to ensure that you are not going over budget on your programme, either through excess of time or on over-delivery of outputs.

All companies which sell time and expertise operate a time-sheeting system. If they don't, the business is not being actively managed and things need to change. This system can either be manually operated or made available to each employee through a more sophisticated project management tool available to each person's desktop.

At the start of a job, your team should have *four management basics* in place and agreed with the client. Your finance director and senior managers will want these to punch into the management accounts, and the office management team will need to know the same numbers, but for purposes of resourcing:

The programme checklist

- A list of deliverables itemising each element of the programme.
- An overall monthly time allocation to be spent on the account by the team.
- A breakdown of those hours by team seniority, i.e. AD, AM, AE, etc.
- Individual team members roles and responsibilities agreed with the client.

Once these building blocks are in place, the following system and process needs to be set up so that your progress is monitored and controlled.

Why? Two clear reasons. It is inexcusable to present clients with badly managed programmes that present nasty surprises about money – this is a sure destroyer of trust, the principal underpinning of productive business relationships. If you can't manage the money, the programme will run away with itself and over servicing – the arch villain of all time-based work – will become like a brush fire: too hot for comfort, uncontrollable and fatally destructive.

Thus, failsafe systems need to be put in place to protect you and your client and foster a productive relationship that aims to build the basis for long-term survival.

The management tools to maximise the chances of this happening may not be the most creative or exciting part of the job, but they provide the envelope in which the programme must be wrapped to ensure a long-term relationship with a client can be developed. It is also the way in which senior management measure managerial and business performance – in this case that means yours!

And, strange though it may seem, clients or in-house bosses will actually respect a manager who negotiates from a position of knowledge and sound business sense. After all, your clients do not work at a loss. They in turn recognise that their agency will hardly be motivated to do a great job on their behalf if they are not making a margin on the work.

The six rules of successful account management

- *MONTHLY PROGRESS REPORTS:* These should be prepared for clients and contain a precise record of the hours spent by each individual on the programme.
- *A RECORD OF ACTUAL HOURS* against projected hours should be attached to every monthly report, providing an audit trail through the

programme. Without this, you have no negotiating position with the client or your department head.

- *A QUARTERY RECONCILIATION OF HOURS* and programme deliverables should be made and discussed with the client as an agenda item at a regular team meeting.
- *A SIX MONTHLY REVIEW*: Build this into the contract to allow for formal renegotiation of hours and deliverables so that you and your team are not locked into an unprofitable arrangement. If over-servicing is rife, it could mean cutting down on the deliverables in the programme, or changing the way you do things. Either way, an unprofitable status quo is not an option.
- *BE PREPARED TO GIVE BACK:* The review should be a two-way street. In other words, if you are getting through a programme using less time than allocated, you should be prepared to hand something back to the client, either by returning cash or by adding further deliverables to the programme. Much as it may hurt to do so, your reputation will rise in direct relationship to the pain.
- *ANNUAL REVIEW*: This should be formally built into the client contract to allow for comprehensive renegotiation or adjustment of terms. The review mentioned above should also be formalised as a selling point.

Using numbers to motivate the team

We all want to work with highly motivated people. They inspire, achieve, enthuse and go after things in a big way. *Strong motivation is a turn on!*

For department heads or team leaders, managing people to ensure that they maintain motivation is a central part of the job. Most people, even highly motivated ones, are eventually turned off by poor management, rather like children are by poor teaching.

Even where they are unable to articulate precisely what poor management is, they know it when they experience it. Getting the job done can sometimes be difficult enough, but a manager who doesn't know what is happening, can't rectify a destructive situation or who fails to defend his team with the client or senior managers, is on the fast track to nowhere.

Time to do things properly is central to everyone's ability to work productively. Underchallenged and motivation drops; overworked and motivation also drops. Though it may sometimes seem like a conjuring trick, a happy medium has to be found if staff are to remain motivated to do their best. The following represents a pathway to ensure that your team recognise why sound financial management can benefit them as a positive force in the workplace.

- *FILL IN TIMESHEETS*: Everyone should fill in time sheets either daily or weekly, never later than that. Explain that time sheets may be a pain, but they are neither a weapon nor a punishment, rather an essential lever for active management. They conceal hidden riches!
- *AVOID WORK OVERLOAD*: Make sure each member of the team knows their allocated hours on each project or account. Also check with senior managers so that you can tell each team member definitively how many billable hours they have each month. In this way, work overload is avoided or restricted.
- *ESTABLISH CLEAR LINK TO PERFORMANCE*: Staff need to know that work which is delivered to time and budget will be rewarded, either financially through promotion or other recognition. This link should be unequivocal and delivered as advertised.
- *EXPLAIN BONUS SCHEMES*: Speak to senior managers to ensure you understand how the company bonus or reward system works. What proportion relates to divisional or team performance and how does it impact on each individual? Make sure your team understands the relationship and what's in it for them.
- *EMPHASISE CAREER SKILLS*: The ability to monitor and control workflows and programmes is an essential part of career development. Without it, the glass ceiling will be set much lower in the workplace.
- *SUPPORT INDIVIDUAL DEVELOPMENT*: If staff are having problems mastering management principles, talk to the HR Department and see what internal or external support may be available. Maybe a session with senior managers internally, or some bought in support could help.
- *MENTOR AND NURTURE*: It's a reality that people sometimes need help and support, even if to reinforce something they know to be true. Build into your management schedule time to spend, perhaps quarterly, with people for whom you are responsible. Go out for a sandwich and a cup of coffee and do some active listening!

Case study 1

The Group is a business-to-business provider of personal general insurance, motoring assistance and other motor related products in the UK. Its products and services include creditor, motor, home, pet and travel insurance as well as motoring assistance and vehicle related services.

To increase the awareness of The Group motoring assistance brand, it sought to ally itself with an emerging issue that crossed all regional, social and demographic boundaries and would be supported by key stakeholders including client companies. Road safety was chosen as a supported cause above issues such as the rising cost of motoring, environmental effects of driving, road building, speeding fines and safer car design because as an issue it affects most of the population and avoids potential conflict with client companies such as motor manufacturers and retailers.

Execution and implementation

The Group agreed to sponsor Road Safety Week and use the national launch event as a platform for the findings of its own research report into road safety. The week and the activities in the lead-up, aimed to raise awareness of the extent of death and injury on the road and explain to people how to improve their own safety.

Activity	Channel/Media	Audience	Timing
Provide briefing to management (research published)	Team Brief	The Group managers	Email briefing 1 March
Article for The Flagship	Internal magazine	Employees	Pre-event article March and follow-up in April
Web page dedicated to Brake	www.flag.com	Visitors	Launched 1 April
Media Relations: target company car drivers with relevant findings	Motoring trade and consumer press	Company car drivers (M/F)	Embargoed releases issued 30 March to target media
Women drivers	Web sites Women's editors (national/regional press)	All women drivers	As above
Target young drivers	Consumer magazines Music station news	Ages 17-21 years	As above
Research findings launch	Breakfast briefing for journalists and report presentation	Media	Morning launch at event in London

COSTING EXERCISE 2:

Use the two tools in this chapter, *Fig One: Fee Rate Calculator* and *Fig 2: Deliverables Calculator* to see if you can cost the programme set out below in the 'Factor It In' PR programme. This time we want one chart that sets out the cost of the deliverables and a second chart that sets out the required amounts of fees, at different levels of the consultancy team, required to input the time required on the account. Inasmuch as is possible, we want the cost of the deliverables to match the cost of the time; the more they reconcile, the more accurate our costings will be. Remember to allocate a percentage of the budget to cover the expenses required to implement the campaign. This budget is spread over 12 months, so you might also want to see if you can make the deliverables and the time match the monthly retainer we would charge to do the whole job.

Case study 2

'Factor It In' campaign
Budget £70,000

Background

Group Factors is a leading UK independent factoring organisation. The company works with the small and medium-sized business community to provide flexible finance solutions designed to overcome cash flow problems and fund growth.

The 'Factor It In' campaign was developed by the PR Consultancy to position Group Factors as an authoritative industry voice with an in-depth understanding of the small business market. The underlying message has been that, in order to succeed, SMEs must get the 'business basics' right. This is what the campaign delivered:

Execution and implementation

Media Relations

A media relations campaign, focusing on the small business pages of the national press, regional and national business publications, financial and accountancy press and key vertical sector press was implemented. In order to 'create' news, the PR Consultancy developed a number of media platforms including a series of seasonal press releases, reacting to topical issues (such as the Chancellor's Budget), and developing tips and advice on key business finance issues.

'Factor It In' booklets

A series of 'Factor It In' booklets were developed, copy written and designed. The booklets were designed with the aim:
- To position Group Factors as industry experts, committed to the SME market.
- To provide an effective media platform with which to generate coverage.
- To provide a useful giveaway for Group Factors' sales force.
- To be distributed to key business organisations such as Business Links, Chambers of Commerce etc.

Spotlight newsletter

The *Spotlight* newsletter was developed as a mechanism by which Group Factors could communicate on a regular basis with its database of 10,000 business advisors and accountants. *Spotlight* has been designed to offer real value and interest to its readers and sources regular contributions from high profile third parties. The success of *Spotlight* led to the introduction of *Small Business Spotlight*, a bi-annual insert, which targets SMEs directly.

Research surveys

Research is always an effective way in which to generate positive press coverage and 'own' an issue. The PR Consultancy negotiated in-magazine surveys to be run in conjunction with two leading publications; *Mind Your Own Business* and *Export Times*. The surveys cover topical small business and exporting issues respectively. The results were published in each magazine and were then used as the basis of press releases distributed to the wider media.

Strategic alliances

Strategic alliances with appropriate partners serve to enforce the credibility and authority of a brand. Group Factors identified the University for Industry (UFI) as a potential partner. The government initiative has been set up to encourage adult learning online and hosts specialist SME courses. The UFI has agreed to use Group Factors guides as a resource for its business learners and in the autumn new Group Factors' clients will be offered free UFI training.

CHAPTER THREE

New Business Development

Introduction; setting sales targets; differentiation and USPs; sales and marketing strategy; setting out your credentials; the classic credentials presentation; constructing an effective pipeline; managing objections; managing the sales operation: exercises.

Introduction

Growing caterpillars need to eat. It is axiomatic that you cannot survive as a PR consultant unless you can pull in and successfully service business. Talking up a storm only goes so far. At some point you have to generate opportunities to show what you can do by getting in front of *a prospect,* someone you are targeting with your business offer, and converting them into a client. In other words, you have to turn opportunities and great ideas into revenue.

One of Britain's most famous and successful advertising men, David Ogilvy, was unequivocal about the central role of sales in building success for the creative industries. "In the modern world of business, it is useless to be a creative, original thinker unless you can also sell what you create. Management cannot be expected to recognise a good idea unless it is presented to them by a good salesman," he said. To that end, the most successful PR consultants are experts in selling. They know just how to package themselves up and make their organisations, their ideas and their people more attractive than the opposition. In an unforgiving business, much like sport, there are no prizes for finishing second. But how do they do this?

The immediate answer is by developing a quality product in which they believe absolutely, understanding the basics of selling and how to set up an effective sales pipeline. In fact, learning how to *sell yourself,* your company and your services is one of the most important personal and professional skills you will ever develop, permeating more aspects of your life than might immediately appear obvious.

It is fair to say that the British have traditionally been open to caricature through their self-effacing and even apologetic approach to talking about money. Nowhere is this trait more exposed than in the process of selling something. Others are not so inhibited; the American culture embraces the salesman and the sales process as a vital and even honourable component of the commercial landscape, even making a science out of customer service and complaints handling. There is no behaviour, though, that cannot be learned.

I have put together this chapter to help both PR newcomers and professionals understand how to develop a more planned, cohesive and successful sales and business development strategy. Even if you are a natural salesperson, it cannot hurt your chances to inject some methodology into your already inspirational performance. If you are not a natural, then acquiring technique and methodology to help drive your work and revenue stream may be the best route to upping your comfort zone and hit rate.

I strongly believe that successful sales people are good communicators. The best communicators talk in simple, effective language and engage their audiences directly. However, they need to be telling a credible story based on a solid, consistent *sales proposition*. Central to this is exploring and agreeing what your story and proposition is all about. It is the companies that cannot define their proposition which become 'me too' organisations, with nothing special or remarkable about them, and therefore generally doomed to obscurity and eventual failure.

What's more, to develop skills in the PR business, you have to become adept at working out what other people's Unique Selling Points (USPs) are too. If you cannot achieve that, it is hard to see what value you can add in helping them get their products and services to market. To that extent, a general understanding of business, organisational dynamics, markets, product cycles, consumer habits and a wider raft of business basics are all extremely important in establishing your credibility and enabling you to talk with authority in a Boardroom.

Setting sales targets

To become real, a *sales pipeline* has to exist within the context of an overall sales target. Targets are especially important because they are a powerful motivator. Accurate measurement of the sales effort is important to resourcing, budgeting and deployment of that effort. No sales plan or forecast should therefore be seen as static, but adaptable to markets and circumstances. This is one way of looking at target-setting when constructing a pipeline:

Sales achieved last year

Measure the new business the consultancy achieved last year, by client number, by revenue and as a percentage of total revenue generated.

Sales forecast for upcoming financial year

Set new business targets for the next financial year. Do you have a sales forecast? The forecast needs to show existing and projected new business, plotted in month by month.

Projected growth increase (%)

To find a realistic growth target, look back over the last five years. By what average percentage has the business grown in revenue terms? How many clients do you have now, and how many did you have three years ago? That average sets a benchmark figure to aim for.

Differentiation and USPs

Differentiation, the process of defining what makes you distinct from your competitors, is at the heart of successful marketing and selling, whether for organisations or individuals. The sales proposition encapsulates what you and your services have to offer the market, the associated USPs set out the separate features and benefits that distinguish your offer from the competition's.

EXERCISE: To see how this works, try to set out below a sales proposition and supporting USPs for a PR consultancy which would make it distinctive. It could be one you are working for already or it might be one you know about. If you can't do this, try and apply the exercise to your own skills,

---

talents and situation – what differentiates you in the workplace? Aim to try and isolate at least three separate USPs. *Compare your answers with an alternative in Chapter Thirteen*

My sales proposition:

Supporting USPs:

Sales and marketing strategy

What is your strategy to make the new business target? Will you focus on targeting prospects by sector, by size or by product? Will you package up your existing services or launch new ones to create new opportunities? A sales strategy that stands a chance of success means being proactive, not reactive. It is important to set out the strategy, even in short form, as it articulates your approach to getting in front of the types of organisation you want to work for.

See if you can find out and articulate your company's sales strategy using no more than five bullet points.

Setting out your credentials

Effective selling, like communications, needs to package and deliver consistent key messages about the product, its USPs and reasons to purchase. Prospects can be better convinced to buy if they can see evidence – demonstrable proof – of your business solutions in action.

This approach works best when they can see how someone else in a comparable position to them has benefited from using your services, for example through the use of *case studies* (see Chapter Seven: Wider and Deeper With Features), sometimes called customer stories. The proof that you assemble to show this is an important part of your presentation and should be showcased effectively in your credentials.

How are you currently presenting your credentials? Are you satisfied with what you are saying about yourself and the story it tells? Is it reasonable to suppose that your current credentials presentation could be at very least updated, at best drastically improved to reflect the reality of your service portfolio and client base?

The classic credentials presentation

So often, credentials presentations miss the target and are a wasted opportunity. A productive way to think about how you might present yourself is to visualise it from the prospect's point of view. Do they want to hear about your many industry awards, office locations and relationships with key journalists, or would they rather hear about themselves, and what you can do to push them further down the road to success or solve a particular problem?

Would they rather wade through copy slide after copy slide of your rise to fame or focus on something about themselves that they may not have known and which you can help fix? Many sales professionals use the concept of needing to know the root cause of someone's pain before coming up with the kind of game plan that means anything to them.

Six slides to say it all

A productive way to think about this challenge is to set yourself a limit rather than see a credentials presentation as being open-ended. For example, if you only had time to present six slides in order to convince a prospect that you were worth putting on their pitch list, which slides would you pick and why? This is a variation of the one-minute *elevator pitch* and is significant in that it focuses the mind on identifying the key elements that would persuade an audience in the given situation.

As both a seller and buyer of PR services, I can confirm that this credentials presentation is a critical first step in the selling process and needs customisation and thought every time. A tip which helps to anchor the process is to ask the question: what would your business look like after one year with us? How would it be changed?

Think about this approach below and benchmark it against your own, for example:

Slide 1	Five ways in which your organisation can change or improve based on our initial analysis of business intelligence and audience habits.
Slide 2	Five ways that we can impact your business performance in our first year as your PR agency.
Slide 3	The measurable value that we could add to that improved performance spread across a mix of metrics, for example behaviours, attitudes, media penetration, digital traffic.
Slide 4	A summary of other people we have helped, how we have helped them and where they are now as a result.
Slide 5	What we do, how we do it differently and how we are more effective than the competition.
Slide 6	Our people – our team, our company, our resources.

Constructing an effective pipeline

For a company to grow, the new business function needs to be systematic, not occasional. Once you get a taste of success, or become immersed in getting a new account off the ground, don't make the mistake of letting up on new business. An effective sales pipeline is one that works all the time, providing a constant input of new leads at one end, as dead wood drops out of the other.

Sales pipelines are constructed around a sales cycle that comprises four separate parts; each component needs to be carried out in balance with each other. Your sales planning & execution strategy needs to accommodate these four elements:

PROSPECTING	PITCHING	CLOSING	TRACKING

PROSPECTING

You should be aiming to identify and contact up to *three new sales prospects* to add to your sales database every week. These contacts can be generated by a combination of actions, for example:

-Networking
-News reports (job moves, key appointments)
-Annual reports
-Industry press
-The Web
-Social media sites such as Linked In; Facebook;
-Bought-in lists

By far the most significant business development activity you can undertake is to network. Successful businesses get most work through referral and recommendation, but it is the capacity to go out and be where your potential clients are that is often the difference between the ordinary and extraordinary new business performance.

When you identify your prospects, you should be aiming to contact them with the objective of getting information in front of them and fixing a face-to-face meeting. You need to exercise judgement to develop the most appropriate ways of doing this, but use a combination of:

-Phone call
-Introductory letter (you can top & tail)
-Personalised e-mail

Before you call or write, make sure you can prove you know and understand the nature of their business and can see a way to add value. Where possible, anticipate objections.

PITCHING

All the groundwork on pitching and closing is done *before* the meeting. Your credentials presentation should be tailored as much as possible to meet any brief you have been given, to showcase your proposition and USPs and to reflect the difference your work has made.

When you get face to face with a potential client, it is up to you to have researched their financial position and potential spend, have checked out their digital footprint through the web and social media, know who the decision-makers are and, as much as possible, have looked into what they are currently doing in their marketing and PR. The final link in the chain is to spend some time anticipating what their objections might be, for example, to your experience, your size, your resources and so on.

In the PR business, you will almost invariably be asked to produce a proposal with creative ideas and a strategic approach to the specific PR and communications challenge you have been asked to address (see Chapter Four: Writing Winning Proposals). Sometimes your pitch will be an opportunity to showcase the content of your proposal, at other times it may combine the presentation and proposal in one step.

CLOSING

As with every other competitive endeavour, coming second hurts just as much every time.

Even the industry heavy hitters don't win all the time. However, you should be aiming for no less than a *one in three* conversion rate, even if that means winning a one-off project rather than a retainer. Whilst the buyer of PR and marketing services is usually a sophisticated audience, he or she is happily not immune to sales techniques that are skilfully applied. Closing a sale is where the real pros shine. The object is to make it impossible for the prospect to say 'no', by reducing his choices to the only logical one – you.

Richard Denny, in his book Selling To Win*, sets out basic rules which he says underpin every sales challenge and which everyone trying to sell products or services would do well to remember. The market for buying and selling PR services is an increasingly mature one; it is certainly not like selling double glazing or second-hand cars. However, buyers still make purchasing decisions using the same basic principles as everyone else.

Among the rules that characterise any sales closing process, it is worth remembering some of the fundamentals, for example that people buy from people so that it pays to become a people expert; likewise, you should cultivate the art of listening and focus on selling the benefits of a product or service rather than the features. In the end, you need to be clear and able to communicate the

Selling To Win, Richard Denny, Kogan Page, 1988.

advantages of your PR services and solutions over the competition; be confident, you don't simply have to be the cheapest to get the business, so avoid the notion of discounting.

TRACKING

This is an essential part of systematic selling and requires the time and effort to set up and monitor a means of tracking your prospects through the sales cycle so that the pipeline remains dynamic.

Use a knowledge management system, (simple spreadsheet or more sophisticated sales database such as ACT or Filemaker Pro) to input sales and marketing data that tracks your meetings through the four part sales cycle, positioning the lead progressively in terms of its conversion potential:

STEP ONE:	First contact (25%): Register interest with follow-up action point
STEP TWO:	Second contact: (50%): Face to face credentials presentation or in-depth telecon with commitment in principle to progress, based on a brief received
STEP THREE:	Third contact: (75%): Detailed proposal submission and team presentation
STEP FOUR:	Fourth contact (100%): Sale agreed – forward plan discussed

The tools to do the job

To sell effectively, the PR consultant needs a basic toolkit which will showcase the business in a way that makes the offer clear, convincing and attractive. There are variations, more often than not budget driven, as to how this showcase is put together, but these days I believe there is a basic must-have toolkit to cover every selling situation.

Second generation website	Provides a 24/7 shop window and information hub for the business. Doesn't have to be fancy, but at least should show the offer, key people, case studies, contact details and Twitter feed.
Corporate PPT	A Powerpoint presentation that works on a tablet and acts as a sales presenter in any face to face selling situation. Comprises proposition, USPs, services, clients, case studies, key people.
Flyer/mailer	Catch-all DL sized mailer which could be enclosed with a letter, used as a leave-behind or placed on an exhibition stand. Good for key messages and summary of services.
Case studies	Long & short versions, with client verification which authenticate your work on given projects and set out the solutions, benefits and thinking that makes you unique.
Media coverage	Where media coverage is concerned, you need to *show*, not just talk about the results you have got for clients. Scanning in some choice cuttings to use in flyers, on a website or in a PPT is a good investment.

Managing Objections

Handling and countering objections successfully is intrinsic to successful selling; all professional salesmen will go through training in how to manage objections, either on the phone or face to face. Preparing for objections should be a process gone into *before* each sales meeting, with judgements made on merit. Remember the three-stage process to deflect objections:

Stage 1: ASK BACK	Find out if what is being said is the real objection (the so-called 'apple' or 'core').
Stage 2: AGREE AND OUTWEIGH	Agree with the thought process, but not with the objection itself. The idea is to establish rapport.
Stage 3: PROVIDE THE ANSWER	Answer the question to the prospect's satisfaction.

Examples of some of the more common objections and counters I have met and used when selling PR consultancy services:

OBJECTION: "PR doesn't work for me."

Agree & outweigh: "I appreciate your view. But what is your direct experience? What have you expected to achieve?"

Provide the answer: "You have never tried a sustained PR campaign before. PR is not a short term fix; it requires some commitment and strategic thinking. Let me tell you a bit about how we work and show you some of the results we have been getting for clients of your kind of size and budget."

OBJECTION: "PR is too expensive."

Agree and outweigh: "Budget is clearly an issue. But too expensive in relation to what? How could you reach your target audiences more cost effectively and with better results?

Provide the answer: "It doesn't have to be. We are very competitive in terms of the audience profile we can reach. And PR services can be scaleable; we offer a range of options, starting with a simple Press Office operation and progressing to a more complex service."

OBJECTION: "PR is too woolly; I don't know what I am buying and I can't measure the results."

Agree and outweigh: "You're right to raise the issue of evaluation. But with PR you need to be clear about what you are paying for and what results you expect to get. Did you have an agreed set of metrics in place?"

Provide the answer: "There are highly effective ways of measuring impact. We can be very precise about what you will get for your money; in fact, we will sign up to very specific criteria for return on investment as part of any contract we enter into between us."

Exercise: see if you can work out a way of countering these further 'classic' objections:

OBJECTION 1:
I've never used PR before. Convince me that it offers value for money and I might change my mind.

OBJECTION 2:
PR doesn't increase sales. I'd rather spend the money on a new salesperson.

OBJECTION 3:
You don't know my business. So what value can PR add to it?

OBJECTION 4:
I only want to pay for results. Will you work on a results achieved basis?

OBJECTION 5:
Media coverage doesn't achieve anything for me. What good is seeing my name in the papers?

OBJECTION 6:
I don't have time to spend taking a PR agency up the learning curve. My strategy is to recruit and develop in-house people.

Managing the sales operation

Processes & Best Practice

To build and develop an effective sales pipeline presupposes a number of process driven changes in your organisation. They are not difficult to set up but, as with any management challenge, success depends on commitment, tenacity and organisation.

Consultancies will generally appoint one person – the *new business manager* – to take control of the sales and business development process. This person should be invested by senior managers with the authority to make things happen and drive the business development programme forward. The new business activity, therefore, requires a 'priority' tag which means it can override account handling when needs must.

If you are a sole practitioner, then you need to recognise that you must take responsibility yourself for moving new business activity from a reactive, or occasional, process to a systematic one. Create half a day a week, for example, when you focus exclusively on executing your sales strategy and new business plan.

The new business manager should, if the organisation is large enough, move away from account handling to focus exclusively on generating and converting leads. The ideal candidate is a very sales driven personality with experience of PR consultancy, not an easy person to locate. The new business portfolio should include:

SALES PIPELINE	Responsibility for setting up and managing the pipeline, from prospecting to reporting.
PRESENTATIONS	Setting up, attending and nominating teams to attend credentials presentations and pitches.
TOOLKIT	Advice, input into and implementation of the corporate sales kit, including website, presenters, flyers, etc.
MANAGEMENT MEETINGS	Weekly meetings with the MD, directors and other senior managers to discuss highlights of the programme and actions required on content and performance.
INCENTIVES	Financial reward, based on commission or other structure, to motivate and reward success.

Databases & Tracking mechanisms

When it comes to monitoring, tracking and reporting systems to manage your pipeline, there are a mass of options. I strongly recommend that any new business tracking mechanism is based on an electronic contact management system. Whilst this may often have excess functionality, it will at least provide the necessary framework for a meaningful business development operation, with data inputs, outputs and consolidated reports.

Within the mass of electronic options available, you can of course get one off the shelf, or have one customised at a relatively low cost to meet your own requirements. For the smaller sales operation, the following are possibilities:

- Access database system, provided by Microsoft and available in the 'Professional' or higher editions of MS Office, or available separately.
- Filemaker Pro, a sales and inventory system which can be adapted to either contact management or project management.
- The ACT contact management system, produced by Sage and arguably the world's best selling electronic tool of its type.

EXERCISE: Build your own brand

Using the six slide formula, see if you can build a presentation that effectively sells your single greatest asset, you. Think about the proposition you offer the market, and the skills and attributes which together differentiate you from others. Try and develop a picture of yourself that a prospective client or an employer might want to see. If you can do that, go one step further and develop a one-minute elevator pitch that packages and sells your brand in a compelling way. This is not easy, but it is interesting to see how you get to grips with this very basic, though essential form of selling.

CHAPTER FOUR

Writing Winning PR Proposals

Adding value; 10-step plan; setting measurable objectives; metrics & evaluation; traditional metrics; new metrics; audiences & messaging; answering the strategy question; tactics & your PR programme; creativity & the 'sizzle factor'; finding the right team; putting a programme in a timeline; budgeting; the contract; exercises.

Once you have sold a prospect on the idea of your credentials and your skills, it would be comforting to think that all the hard work has been done. Not so. In fact, it is only just beginning.

You are now moving into the proposal and pitching phase where your strategic insight, creative ideas, leverage of networks and tactical approach must single you out from others who are chasing the same prize.

Sometimes the challenge is combined into a single exercise, the proposal and pitch in one go, perhaps simply set out in a Powerpoint presentation with a commentary. More often than not, though, you will need to put together your ideas in a formal proposal which gives the detail of your response to the brief. It is this proposal which must contain the rigorous thinking, sector or product knowledge, creative ideas and detail which will differentiate you from your competitors.

Proposals, like everything else, benefit from the application of a method in line with best practice. It is one thing to be judged against the competition on the basis of a level playing field, it is quite another to be disadvantaged simply because you have forgotten to cover one of the critical bases. So, the first thing to learn about proposals is that you must protect against the downside of a procurement department ruling you out simply on the basis of a box you have forgotten to tick. This chapter has been put together partly to ensure against the error of omission.

We have already heard that buyers often make their decisions based on emotion, rather than logic. That may be true. But institutional buyers also make purchasing decisions based on a range of boxes that need ticking. Not least of these is price. For many years now, the procurement departments of large corporates have endeavoured to commoditise PR services in such a way that they can be bought by the yard, using the same process deployed to buy widgets.

Thus price remains a powerful influence on buying decisions, as does size. The same organisations will sometimes exert pressure to buy PR services from the biggest company in the pitch. Why? Because, if the campaign is not 100 per cent successful, the buyer will always be able to say they didn't take a chance on an outsider, but went with the biggest and the most proven brand. This default position, though corrosive, is not uncommon. Regardless then of the creative content of your proposal, the envelope within which it is constructed must conform technically.

Step One: Adding value

Your PR proposal must start off with a bang, not a whimper. To do this, you cannot simply restate the PR brief you have been given, perhaps by summarising its key points. You have to go further and say more. You do this through adding strategic insight and business intelligence and, above all, by showing the prospect something about themselves that they don't already know. This is where the process of consultancy really starts.

One way of giving your proposal its vital strategic context is by shaping your communications plan as a solution to a business problem or an enabler of an opportunity, or combination. The trick here is never to accept a brief at its face value – always make the opportunity to talk to the prospect face-to-face or on the phone about the brief and ask questions which will tell you more about what lies behind the words on the page.

It may seem obvious, but your PR plan is going to fall at the first hurdle if it does not have an immediate strategic context in support of the commercial goals of the business. Thus, if the business is expanding its footprint into new geographies, it makes sense that the focus of the PR should be to create corporate and product awareness in those new markets; if, on the other hand, the issue is that the business can't seem to retain its customers, then the PR solution would seem to coalesce around a customer support communications programme which binds those customers more tightly to the organisation.

This approach will yield dividends because of its strategic, rather than tactical, focus. To support this approach there are a range of auditing and research tools which consultancies will use to develop a situational analysis of a business and its internal and external environments. The standard tool for internal analysis is the SWOT (Strengths, Weaknesses, Opportunities, Threats); the standard for external analysis is the PEST (Political, Economic, Social, Technological, sometimes supplemented by the Legal and Environmental audit, making PESTLE).

Together with a deeper interrogation of the brief and a strategic approach to the communications challenge, these two research tools will shape a map of the internal and external environments within which your PR plan must operate. A full communications audit will extend this process to an analysis of the channels and outputs a business uses across its communications and PR function.

Focusing your thinking at the front end of a proposal is critical. If you cannot show that you have understood the business and the dynamics of its operating environment, you cannot credibly put forward a response which goes beyond a kneejerk, tactical PR plan. When starting out your PR proposal, bear in mind the following simple equation:

Market Intelligence + Insight = Added Value

Step Two: Setting measurable objectives

There is an old saying in the PR world, that if you aim at nothing you are going to hit it. Orthodox thinking these days about PR programmes is very different than it used to be. It is no longer acceptable to have a general objective, for example, 'to generate press coverage'. We now need to know precisely what level of coverage, and in which target media, even drilling down into whether the coverage is positive, negative or neutral, or if the correct key messages are carried.

A general truth when setting objectives is that, if PR wants to be taken seriously in the boardroom, it has to prove that it adds value. Therefore, where possible, this value now needs to be expressed as a Return on Investment (ROI). This step is designed to move PR conceptually from being an overhead – its traditional spot in the budget cycle – to being a net contributor to the bottom line. As you may imagine, this is not always easy to do, but American practitioners such as Angela Sinickas are coming up with new models that increasingly set out to articulate just such an idea (www.sinicom.com).

But what goals can PR achieve that can authentically be expressed as added value? There are a number of general answers to this question, which together make public relations such a powerful modern business tool. It is a range of measures which, taken as a whole, no other business discipline can match.

Value that PR can add to organisations

- Market awareness and visibility
- Leadership positioning
- Enhanced reputation
- Third party endorsement, credibility
- New relationships and partnerships
- Sales leads and enquiries
- Stakeholder engagement
- New business opportunities
- Media profile
- Behaviour and attitude change

These goals collectively answer the question 'why bother to do PR?' But nowadays, when we set PR objectives, wherever possible the name of the game is to generate measurable change in either attitudes, or behaviours, or both. This means, through our communications, that we ask our target audience to do something, to not do something or do something differently; in the case of behaviours, this is sometimes referred to as *'call to action'* campaigning and has been most prevalent in the public and charity sectors. Having this kind of change as a target has a certain beauty, which is that behaviour change can be precisely measured, say for example, through the number of hits on a website or the number of calls to a hotline that result from PR activity.

Of course, behaviour change cannot be the objective of every PR campaign or indeed tactic, so where are the fertile business areas in which to look for realistic objectives? These coalesce around a number of outcomes, typically:

Influence: coverage of key positive messages in primary target press
Relationship building: face-to-face briefings and meetings
Knowledge: increase consumer awareness of our brand or product

Reputation: increase our reputation index score
Sales: support increase in sales of x %
Employee engagement: increase volunteers for our CSR programme, for example
Product: increase use of specific product Y amongst current customers

Again, orthodox thinking from professional bodies such as the Chartered Institute of Public Relations (CIPR) now dictates that all PR objectives need to be set out in line with the SMART principle – *Specific, Measurable, Achievable, Realistic and Timely.* This principle of objective setting travels across many forms of consultancy, not just public relations, but offers a good general reference point.

So, when setting out your objectives the trick is to spread them perhaps across a range of different parameters and, for example, set one that directly supports the sales effort, one that deepens audience understanding, a further one that establishes new relationships and perhaps a media driven one that aims for press coverage. This kind of mix would constitute a good generic balance. In any event, the objectives should relate precisely to the aim of the programme or campaign.

Step Three: Metrics & evaluation

There is a hoary old cliché in business which states: "If you can't measure it, you can't manage it!" This mantra may be accused of confined thinking these days but, like all clichés, it contains a kernel of truth.

Setting objectives makes your PR campaign real. You are now aiming for outcomes which achieve added value for an organisation. But your progress towards these outcomes cannot be verified without associated metrics that show to what degree you have been successful. Agreeing on meaningful and affordable metrics is a vexed question and one which the PR profession is spending a great deal of time, energy and resources on answering.

What is true is that there is not yet a perfect solution to this question and, until that changes, the PR profession is going to have a problem getting a permanent seat at the boardroom table. However, the position is fluid and organisations such as the Association of Media Evaluation Companies (AMEC), through its Barcelona Principles and others, are making progress in defining the answers for the wider industry (www.amec.org).

Where does that leave PR consultants seeking watertight answers to the measurement and evaluation problem? The answer is with a range of traditional and new metrics to choose from, making sure that each objective set out in the PR plan has an associated metric. Taking this approach means your PR proposal will never be open to the accusation: 'where is the value and the proof of results?' Both will be explicit and signed up to before the plan becomes a programme.

Underpinning the developing science of evaluation in PR is the principle that you can measure three specific and related results:

- Outputs: what you actually produce, i.e. numbers of news releases or press briefings
- Out takes: results – in media relations, for example, where your story was covered in target media
- Outcomes: what the target audiences did as a result of your communications.

As a methodology, this is a good starting point for planning your evaluation as it focuses on three specific measures.

Traditional metrics

Metrics traditionally used in PR evaluation include those borrowed from advertising alongside those unique to PR. For example:

ADVERTISING:

- Audience surveys and polls
- Cost per thousand (or CPM) = cost of reaching 1,000 people in target market
- Opportunities To See (OTS) = number of times an audience is exposed to one message/ad = effective reach
- Direct Response: sales leads and enquiries

PUBLIC RELATIONS:

- Advertising Value Equivalence (AVE)* = cost of advertising space with weighting for third-party endorsement

*Though AVEs are now officially discredited, they are sometimes still used.

- Direct Response: sales leads and enquiries generated through editorial coverage
- Pre and post campaign awareness surveys

Advertising Value Equivalence (AVE) example

A measure originally developed to add a value beyond comparable paid for space by introducing a weighting to reflect the value of third-party editorial endorsement

Cost of full page advertisement in 'People' Magazine:	£5,750.00
Half page editorial (eg: interview with your client CEO)	£2,875.00
Multiple to provide weighting for third-party endorsement	x4
Advertising Value Equivalent (AVE)	£11,500.00

Cost Per Thousand (CPM) Example

Comparative measure of cost-effectiveness in different types of advertising: Calculation: divide cost of an ad by the publication's readership or circulation within the target group

Cost of full page ad in 'People' Magazine	£5,750.00
Circulation	126,000
Cost per thousand	£0.045

PR Surveys: using traditional market research methodologies

Technique: Observational analysis
– *Definition*: Impartial third-party assessment of available media
Technique: Interview
– *Definition*: Open-ended individual discussion
Technique: Focus group
– *Definition*: Open-ended group discussion
Technique: Survey
– *Definition*: Mostly closed-ended questions

New metrics

With the passage of time a wide range of tools and methodologies, many of them *proprietary*, have emerged onto the market with the prime intention of making the process of measurement and evaluation both more sophisticated and more practical. These methodologies, most of which can be customised, require some budget in order to access. However by outsourcing and customising say, evaluation of a media relations campaign, consultancies can now offer a much wider perspective on a range of measures, including, for example, penetration of key campaign messages, tone of coverage being positive, negative or neutral, financial value, and Opportunities To See (OTS).

New media measurement models, such as Google Analytics, contain greater sophistication and a variety of online metrics deployed to measure penetration and traffic of PR activity in the digital and social media space, for example, websites, Facebook, Twitter and other social media channels. These methodologies include:

- Search engine optimisation (SEO) campaigning
- Clicks and Impressions
- Cost per click (CPC)
- Click through rate (CTR)
- Audience reach
- Social media engagement, digital traffic.

The balanced scorecard

When evaluating the contribution or ROI of corporate communications and PR activity, most communications directors will use a mix of evaluation tools and methodologies depending on the kind of programme they are overseeing. This is known as *'the balanced scorecard'* and would include a selection of the methodologies we have looked at here, for example:

- Reputation index score, usually used by larger organisations
- Sales leads & enquiries, where the PR activity can be directly tracked
- Media analysis, including proprietary methods alongside at least one financial measure showing return
- Attitude & awareness surveys

- 'Call to action' outcomes, such as hotline responses or website hits
- Online analytics to measure digital traffic
- Behaviour change, where outcomes can be measured in the context of doing something differently.

Step Four: Audiences and messaging

Your proposal has to be specific about who the communications is directed at. If you cannot isolate the audiences you need to target, you cannot make decisions about the appropriate channels to use and the types of outputs you need to produce. This process is known as *'audience segmentation'* and involves a systematic analysis of an organisation's key stakeholders and influencers. This process, sometimes called stakeholder mapping, can be quite simple or highly sophisticated and can include making decisions about which groups within the audiences have low or high power, or low or high interest.

Once you have isolated your audiences, you have to be very clear and precise about what it is you want to say to them. This associated part of the process is known as *messaging* and messages, or key messages, really constitute the DNA of your communications. Messages represent the essence of what you have to say to each part of your target audience so, for example, your message for shareholders will differ from your message for consumers or your workforce. A message and stakeholder map often travel together, for obvious reasons.

These days, organisations talk about a conversation, or dialogue with their target audiences. And it is true that meaningful communications is a two-way process, the so-called 'two-way street' first introduced by PR pioneer Ivy Lee in the 1920s. Modern communications cannot be about monologue, in effect a cul-de-sac, as this paternalistic style of engagement no longer holds currency. Dialogue, accentuated and increasingly enabled by social media and real-time communications tools, therefore plays a major role in controlling perceptions of a business, its culture, philosophy, values, products, services and people. PR and advertising often take a leading role in developing and delivering the messages that drive this dialogue.

About key messages

Much is talked about messages or 'key messaging' as the process is known. But, in general terms, your messages will not work if they are overly complex or hard to get across. They need to be: simple and meaningful; consistent; memorable; and outward looking. They are, in essence, what you want people to remember as a result of your communications and PR.

The most productive way to think about messaging, is to use a simple matrix. Set out your key message first, then test it by setting out three associated proofs which show that message to be true. Then bring the message to life, make it real for people via an anecdote or story that injects a human dimension. For example, lets say you are a manufacturer of laptop computers and you want to tell your customers that you are the market leader. Your message matrix might look like this:

Target audience: consumers

KEY MESSAGE
"We are the market leader in mobile computing."

PROOFS
1. "We sell more products in more markets than any company in the sector."
2. We have 27 offices in 19 countries."
3. "Our employee numbers topped 25,000 last year."

ANECDOTE/STORY
"Last year we opened an office in Kabul which, by any standards, is a frontier market. Our APACS manager has been shipping product through the Khyber Pass – in winter!"

Once you have locked in this idea, it then becomes a systematic process to develop at least one key message for each of your stakeholders, or target audiences. Once you have agreed them you can then embed the messages in your communications.

Step Five: The strategy question

A major factor in getting ahead in the world of PR consultancy is to be able to think strategically. If you were to accept the hypothesis that the world divides into strategists and tacticians, then it is the tacticians who get stuck in the mud and become simply 'implementers' or doers. As we know, it is the strategists who play a central role in running organisations, by setting out the vision, the mission and the direction and then deciding the overall approach to advancing the interests of the organisation. To progress in PR consultancy, as in any consultancy, you must become a strategic thinker.

Public relations consulting is, by its nature, strategic. It was Edward Bernays, the founder of modern day public relations, who coined the term 'counsel on public relations' to describe the PR practitioner's role sitting next to senior management, giving strategic advice to influence audience behaviours and achieve corporate goals. The PR director is in fact increasingly in the boardroom just because of his or her ability to process business intelligence and give strategic advice.

We have all sat round a table and listened to someone pose the question: "What's the strategy?" Within the context of a proposal, we simply cannot afford not to have an answer to that question. Our proposal brings together the business of consulting with the business of public relations counsel to the point at which we need to have a coherent approach that goes beyond, for example, a basic tactic such as issuing a news release.

Someone once wrote that there are only two strategies, to engage or not to engage. I have seen PR proposals which major on engagement with target audiences as their principal strategic building block. However, we need to take it a little further than that.

You could say strategic thinking starts out by asking some basic questions, for example: what theoretical model of modern communication will you use; what is the mix of communications channels you will deploy; or how will you engage across the audience profile?

First, remember that our role as consultants contributing to senior management decision-making has three principal functions: analysis, advice and action-based programmes. Thus there is an immediate strategic context for our proposed PR programme. We need to add value through market analysis and business intelligence so that we can help senior management better understand their environment; we need to package up advice and tell them what to do before an issue becomes a problem, for example through crisis planning and management, and then we need to implement an agreed PR plan, lets say by setting up and managing an outsourced press office as a media tactic, or setting up a speaker programme as a way of generating profile through our key people.

Communications models

If you study communications theory, you will find underpinning today's PR practice four widely accepted models for corporate communications and PR set out by the respected academics Grunig & Hunt. These models are in some measure relevant to answering the strategy question, as they provide a theoretical underpinning to what kind of conversation we are proposing. It therefore makes sense to locate your PR strategy within one of these models:

Grunig & Hunt: Characteristics of the four models of public relations★

Publicity/press agentry: Propaganda, one-way, truth not essential, little research. Used in product promotion or sponsorship.

Public information: Dissemination of information, one-way, truth important, little research. Used in government and not-for-profit sector.

Two-way asymmetric: Scientific persuasion, two-way but imbalanced effects, using research of attitudes. Used in competitive business.

Two way symmetric: Mutual understanding, two-way and balanced, research of understanding. Used in regulated business.

Some common strategies

It may seem unlikely, but strategy is often expressed quite simply. Think for a moment of George W Bush's re-election strategy, Faith, Flag & Family, that permeated every aspect of his campaign. I would go so far as to say beware of strategy which is too complex to articulate in a simple way. I have assembled and deconstructed many PR proposals and, with time, have seen that the strategic drivers of communications – whilst they may sometimes be difficult to tease out – are not infinite. There is a pattern and after time it becomes apparent that the same strategies come round regularly.

★Grunig & Grunig have suggested that the two-way symmetrical approach is the most ethical and effective way to practice PR. However, they acknowledge that most businesses tend to adopt asymmetrical or public information tactics, or a combination.

Start with the question: what strategic approach will I take on which I can hang effective, affordable and deliverable tactics? Consider these 'classic' PR strategies:

- *Build network capability*: expand your networks so that you can target and talk to more people.
- *Create high value information*: make yourself the first place journalists will go to because they can't access similar high quality information anywhere else.
- *'Own' the issue*: if you are campaigning, then become the most authoritative voice on your issue, for example, as the charity Shelter does with homelessness.
- *Engage*: be where the audience is and be proactive.
- *Create brand experiences*: experiential PR is all about making the brand come to life and letting consumers see and feel it through live interaction.
- *Find and deploy 'champions'*: for example in the way Britain's Olympics 2012 PR campaign used David Beckham, Steve Redgrave and Kelly Holmes to front bid activity.
- *Use leaders to carry the message*: notice, for example, how Virgin uses Sir Richard Branson as the face of the company in all its major PR launches.

Linking strategy to tactics

When putting your strategy together, bear in mind that it only makes sense in context. Strategy, as a concept, sits between your objectives and your tactics. It is therefore sometimes helpful to set up a chain which expresses that relationship explicitly. I would say that there has to be a clear link between objectives, strategy and tactics if your proposal is to be coherent. The more coherent your proposal, clearly the easier it becomes to buy.

Consider the following examples where two separate strategies work towards meeting the same objective:

Strategy One

OBJECTIVE
Create 'expert' positioning

STRATEGY
Generate high value information

TACTICS
Commission fresh research on key issues
Produce a White Paper
Aggregate all facts and statistics into a database
Develop online portal

Strategy Two

OBJECTIVE
Create 'expert' positioning

STRATEGY
Use leaders to carry the message

TACTICS
Create conference speaking programme
Write and place articles in vertical sector press
Implement media training to create more effective spokespeople
Set up press briefings with top five target journalists

Step Six: Tactics and your PR programme

You PR programme, or tactical plan, simply answers the question: 'what are we proposing to do and when?' It includes a number of fixed points, among them your creative ideas, your mix of tools and channels to reach the market, your outputs and a timeline. It is, in other words, a highly practical part of your proposal which is explicit and also a showcase for your professional and technical expertise.

Modern day public relations has an almost infinite number of tactics to deploy, online and offline, media facing or not, face-to-face or remote and highly targeted or widely spread. Each set of PR tactics is purpose-built to meet a specific communications challenge. Your job in your proposal is a clear one – to set out a detailed tactical content, roll-out and timeline, delivering on your strategy and aimed at meeting one or more of your objectives.

To that extent, you could pick from a large toolkit of outputs which you can tailor-make into a highly customised package. Every year, the PR profession seems to get more tools to use, with perhaps the most recent introductions being digital communications, social media and corporate social responsibility (CSR) programmes. The rule when shaping a PR programme is not to use a one-size-fits-all approach but to select only those tools which are appropriate to the task and to the budget. Thus, simply because you are an expert in media relations, don't make the mistake of putting all your PR programmes into a media driven package.

The following checklist is just a reminder of some of the tactical options that are open to you. A typical retained annual PR programme might contain a mix of these tactics, with perhaps an emphasis on media relations as the core activity:
- Sponsorships
- Events, exhibitions
- Seminars, speeches, roundtable meetings
- Media relations: news releases; features; press briefings; position statements and case studies
- A CSR programme
- Newsletters and ebulletins
- Digital media activity, such as blogs, Tweets and Facebook groups
- Original research to underpin your campaign

A good tip when selecting tactics is to look at case studies of award winning campaigns to see what other consultancies have done tactically to deliver on a communications and PR challenge in the same sector. This is not a morally ambiguous suggestion, but we need to be pragmatists. It is helpful to benchmark tactical ideas and create a balance between ambition and practicality.

Looking for precedent and taking it into account makes sense. You can access a wealth of case studies online; perhaps the best starting point is winners of the annual PR PRIDE awards. To access these, visit: www.cipr.co.uk

Step Seven: Creativity & the sizzle factor

I am not proposing to deal in detail here with creativity in PR because it deserves, and already has, a book all to itself, and others are more qualified than

I to unpack the subject. However, it may be valuable to address this issue in the context of your PR proposal by pointing out that some kind of creative content is generally a requirement; remember that part of the purpose and remit of public relations is to disrupt the flow of ordinary events by creating something extraordinary. Just think of Austrian skydiver Felix Baumgartner to test that supposition for a moment. What price would Red Bull Stratos put on its brand recognition and value after his 24-mile plummet to earth tracked by eight million YouTube viewers?

It is almost a truism that clients hire PR consultants because they are able to come up with creative ways to promote organisations which don't, on the surface, sometimes have very much to say. And some agencies are known precisely for their ability to come up with themes, treatments or stunts which, together, can lift the mundane and make it exciting, newsworthy and memorable.

Part of the process of putting your proposal together is to organise at least one *brainstorm* through which you collect all the people in the agency together and think through the creative possibilities and treatments that can shape your communications programme. This process, sometimes formal and sometimes informal, can yield a wealth of fruitful ideas alongside a good helping of dross. The skill is to sort through the outputs of this brainstorming process to isolate those ideas which can be converted from the page to action, because they are practical, affordable and appropriate to the organisation.

Many people in the PR business will go so far as to say that consultancy is attractive to them just because it allows the space in which to be truly creative, and it is true that this is why many people go into PR agencies. However, there is no guarantee that you can come up with creative ideas that are workable all the time. The trick is to work together with others and learn the lessons of creative success by looking closely at case studies which show what has succeeded in the past.

Two examples of how creative thinking ended up with massive coverage:

CHEDDAR VISION TV: a dedicated internet based television channel via which consumers could watch 'Wedginald' a cheddar cheese, mature over a period of months.
http://www.youtube.com/watch?v=VVMt9ECdOjA

T-MOBILE VIRAL VIDEO: Royal wedding viral campaign. A superb video which was a spoof on the wedding of Prince William and Katherine Middleton; attracted over 26 million views alone.
http://www.youtube.com/watch?v=Kav0FEhtLug

Step Eight: Finding the right team

Your proposal needs to be explicit about the team who will work on the business. Not only because you have to 'show' your capability but because above all you need to create the right kind of chemistry. As we have seen when selling, people buy people, they do not necessarily follow a logic but rely on emotion to make decisions.

This part of your proposal needs to be clear about the team and why they have been picked. It also needs to set out their role and say what they will be doing. When choosing from a pool of people, sometimes teams will pick themselves. But at other times they will not and you will need to make judgements about who is most suitable. When selecting teams a useful tip is to make sure you don't pick individuals who all have the same experience and skills. And tailor your choices where possible to the nature of the programme they will be working on. If, for example, the programme is majoring on media relations then it hardly makes sense to pick two events specialists as the daily contacts.

Team building checklist:

Time: Quantify how much you will need in order to produce the outputs indicated in your programme.
Expertise: What level of expertise in the consultancy will you need to allocate the time at: AD, AM, AE?
Skills: Pick people because they each bring something different to the project, rather than doubling up.
Biogs: Produce thumbnail sketches of each person in the team, summarising experience, skills and role.

Step Nine: Budgeting

Much of the territory around budgeting has already been covered in this book and I do not propose to repeat it. Suffice to say that the mathematics has to work as well as the ideas. However it might be worth restating that many purchasers of PR services – procurement departments are just one example – still buy on price. If your prices are too expensive, however attractive your PR solution, you will not make the sale. It is therefore incumbent on you in your proposal to spell out as explicitly as possible the fees and cost estimates that together will make up the budget.

Transparency allows prospects to make a buying decision that is as informed as possible. The less a prospect feels that costs are hidden, the clearer they are about what they are buying. So the clever move is to set out the financials in a way that pre-empts questions and offers reassurance on all the bases that you need to cover.

Your budgeting checklist:

Pricing: What basis are you proposing to work on: retainer or project, or both? Generally project work is priced higher, as the retainer offers agency stability.
Fees: What fees will you charge to get the job done? And at what rates for individuals or deliverables?
Costs: Leave at least 10% of the budget available for costs of implementing the programme.
Estimates: Provide estimates of the bought-in costs required to deliver the outputs: print, websites, and so on.

Step Ten: The contract

Whilst the contract comes into play if you have actually won the business, it is worth stating in your proposal the general terms and conditions that you abide by as a professional organisation. So, if you are a member of a professional body such as the Public Relations Consultants Association (PRCA) or the Chartered Institute of Public Relations (CIPR), it is in your interests to state that you will use a standard contract which sets out the legal basis and Terms and Conditions (T&C) on which your work will move forward.

This sets the tone for the professional relationship that will need to be developed as and when you are taken on. You can use this to flag up any particular issues which may shape your relationship, such as discounting available to clients who spread your work over the course of a year (commonly called a 'retainer') or the other services you might provide as an intermediary, such as design, print and production, or through associated companies.

EXERCISE: INTERROGATE A PR BRIEF

Below is a shortened and reconstituted version of a brief from the Department of Health for the annual PR campaign to promote awareness of the free flu vaccine for certain groups in the UK. Look carefully at this brief and make a note of five different things you could do to add value to your proposal and which you might incorporate into the front end of your proposal document. You do this by setting out business intelligence or insight, or both, in a way that shows you have taken an extra step to unpick the communications challenge and add value. Check your answers against the suggestions in Chapter Thirteen.

DEPARTMENT OF HEALTH FLU AWARENESS CAMPGAIN

Every year the Department of Health (DOH) mounts a flu awareness campaign to alert vulnerable groups to the dangers of contracting flu, combined with the Government offer of a free flu vaccine. Vulnerable groups are classified as: pensioners and the elderly; those with chronic diseases, such as heart conditions or asthma; and some ethnic minority groups who have a very low take-up of health prevention measures. It is also statistically true that many eligible Londoners do not take up the opportunity of a free vaccine.

In addition to consumers, the campaign is aimed at GPs and other medical outlets and centres where consumers can access information about preventive health. Integral to the campaign is the use of a personality to front it up to provide visibility and recall. In this case Billy Walker, one of Britain's best known boxers and sporting personalities, will again be featured on posters and in direct mail leaflets, using the slogan: 'Get Your Jab In First'.

The DOH Press Office will be co-ordinating activity with a network of regional flu advisors around the country, supplying them with information, data and statistics about the illness and the campaign, together with campaign collateral. The objectives of this year's campaign are to increase by 3%, from 72% to 75%, the existing numbers of eligible groups taking up the free vaccine.

The chosen PR company will need to think creatively about ways of leveraging existing campaign strategies rather than reinventing the wheel. Part of the challenge will be to put across a strong national message, but think about ways in which to reach the vulnerable target groups directly. Some of these, specifically some ethnic minority groups, do not access information through conventional English language print and broadcast channels, but may get their information in other ways, for example through community centres and own language radio.

The chosen agency does not necessarily need experience of the health sector, but must show it can think both strategically and tactically in ways which will communicate the campaign message effectively. The agency will be results oriented and required to show clear objectives in its planning and implementation. It will also need to work closely with DOH Press Office, the regional network of flu co-ordinators and a project manager based in London.

The PR budget for the campaign is £70,000. The campaign is expected to run for seven months, beginning in early October and with final evaluation in April 2013. The agency will not be expected to fund research into take-up from this budget; DOH statistics gathering is covered under a separate budget.

CHAPTER FIVE

Media Relations

Introduction; building media lists; delivering the news; online support; planning media relations campaigns; building the media toolkit; online media channels; writing for the web; guide to classic digital outputs; pitching to journalists.

Introduction

Media relations, the business of selling in and placing news stories, features, comment and opinion in the media, analogue and digital, is still the predominant component of most PR programmes. Whether aiming at the nationals, regionals, broadcast or vertical sector press, many PROs spend their time cultivating relationships with journalists and bloggers and getting client information in front of them at the right time. Coverage in the press remains for the moment the most common yardstick by which PR success is measured. What's more, writing and media relations skills are ranked more highly by employers than any others, at 86% and 81% respectively.[*]

Thus, writing for the media is still at the heart of most PR practice. Why is this so? Going back to the 1920s, we can see the first public relations practitioners, men like Ivy Ledbetter Lee and Edward Bernays (see Chapter Twelve, Caterpillars of Wisdom) used media relations as a primary tool in their campaigning. They recognised that the media were gatekeepers to a massive popular, and indeed specialist, audience that together reached the entire consumer demographic. It was Ivy Lee, a former journalist, who was credited with writing the first press release in 1906 on behalf of the Pennsylvania Railroad Company.

Bernays, however, was the first and foremost theorist and philosopher in

[*]Tench & Fawkes 2005

the field and the first to recognise and articulate the power of third-party endorsement. He realised that the media, as an objective and expert body concerned with news, carried huge weight in influencing the opinions and attitudes of a public who he regarded as malleable. Both men recognised the subtleties and nuances that separated the facts from the truth, and were able to access and hijack the mainstream news agenda by clever story selection, presentation and timing.

With it widely accepted today that up to 80% of the work of the typical PR programme still focuses on traditional and new media relations, it therefore follows that knowing how the media works, what journalists want from PRs and how to deliver a written product that is fit for purpose are intrinsic to getting a result.

To make that happen, it helps to adopt the journalistic mindset and create your media outputs with a journalist's head on. In effect, the principles and craft skills of journalism still underpin the expertise that PROs need to develop in order to be effective intermediaries in the news process.

If it is helpful for PR consultants to be able to talk and move in the journalistic world, they also need to master a skill set which is entirely unique to the practice of media relations, from how to put together a media list to some basic rules for pitching stories successfully to news or features editors.

The rules of media relations

1. Don't even begin writing for the media until you start reading the media professionally.
2. Learn to recognise the different formats that work across the media and start deconstructing what shines.
3. Stop thinking like an artist and start thinking like an artisan. To succeed, you need method, so learn it.
4. Respect the journalistic craft… find out what the end-to-end process is all about, from research & news gathering to sub-editing and layout.
5. Understand the dynamics of stories… what are they, where do they come from and how do you find yours?
6. Never write in a vacuum; keep the reader at the front of your mind at all times
7. Get comfortable in your writer's skin. Success breeds success. With practice, you *will* get better, so persist.

---

8. Get to know target journalists personally. Good media relations means good relations with the media.
9. Even if you are not a natural, you can still be professional. Remember that good writing skills are at the heart of much PR success.

Building media lists

Getting the best result from your media relations programme depends on creating the right content and presenting it in the right format. However, that is only doing half the job. The other half depends on making sure it reaches the right person on the right media title when it matters most.

Thus, intelligent research, construction and customisation of media lists means deciding on and targeting the precise kind of publication and correspondent your story will interest. Remember that all publications or broadcast outlets are gatekeepers to their audience – they know what types of news, features, case studies or interviews and profiles will get the readers on the hook.

To build media lists, start by dissecting your target audience. Who are they, where do you find them, and how do they like to get their information? In magazines, on TV or online or, increasingly these days, via their own mobile devices such as ipads and mobile phones. Or through all of these? Use directories and online resources like *Mediadisk* to build your list. At all costs, be sure the names, titles and contact details are up to date – nothing reduces your credibility more with journalists than information being sent to someone who left a publication two years ago.

Through this process, you can build a media matrix that is fully customised for the purpose. Your options might include a mix of:

- *Horizontal press (accessed by your whole demographic) including: nationals; regionals; broadcast media; online;*
- *Vertical sector press (specialist & trade): for example IT and computing: business & management;*
- *Blogs, personal online sites, citizen journalists*
- *News agencies and picture agencies: for example the Press Association (PA) or Reuters; news aggregator sites, such as Yahoo News.*

The media identified in your target list can be approached via a number of entry points: individual journalists who have specific roles and titles, for example, editors, news editors, special correspondents, feature writers, freelancers, researchers and so on.

Delivering the news

Back in the 1980s and early 90s, all news releases were sent in hard copy format using snail mail or, occasionally, fax, a process which today would seem incredible. Now these options have opened up and there is much greater choice of distribution channel. Some publications and individual journalists are very particular about how they get their information, so it pays to do some research into how and when you should send editorial.

It is usually best to use a mix of channels: email, posting to websites, fax, hard copy or phone – they all have their place (see: Pitching to journalists). However, a basic understanding of distribution might include knowing information like the following:

- Daily newspapers really need a story by early afternoon if it is going to make the next day's edition.
- Monthly consumer magazines work up to three months ahead on big features.
- Monthly magazines put their news pages together up to the start of the last week of the preceding month.
- If you are emailing a release to a journalist, it is usually better to put the headline in the email subject box and cut and paste the release itself into the body of the email.

The action point here is to make sure you reach every target journalist in the way *you know* they like to get their information.

Online Support

There are a variety of proprietary systems to help you ramp up the effectiveness of your news and feature delivery and hit rate. These include the Mediadisk journalists database (www.cision.com), Response Source, the online marketplace for journalists and PROs to share news and feature opportunities (www.responsesource.com) and the media database Gorkana (www.gorkana.com); all these products and systems offer scope for the PR practitioner to improve their coverage and their hit rates, combining alerts, smart databases and contact management systems.

When building media databases, make them 'intelligent'. That is to say, you should be in the business of customising your media database for each client by taking into account the record and interests of the individual journalists you are trying to reach. What did they last write about? What are their strongest interests? Knowing this background when you contact them makes a massive difference to your reception.

Planning media relations campaigns

When people talk of a media relations strategy, what do they really mean? In general terms, this implies developing a plan which is going to deliver the maximum amount of exposure, column inches and enquiries for your product or message across all target media read by your campaign audiences. This means knowing the target media well and maximising the possibilities offered by the different media channels – print, broadcast and online – so that content, timing and distribution of your media outputs generate the maximum return possible.

Thus, a highly evolved media relations strategy will combine a mix of tactics and outputs, all timed for maximum effect. This mix could include press briefings, news releases, multimedia news releases (MNRs), photo-opportunities, profiles, feature-length pieces or byelined articles, with content sliced and diced to meet corporate, product and people-based agendas.

But looking a little deeper, your media relations strategy covers a number of other areas. For example, using current national, regional or industry issues to provide news and feature leverage; if you are a high street bank, promoting a new mortgage offer on the back of house purchase figures or interest rate hikes, for example; or, as a manufacturer of domestic security equipment working into your story the latest official figures on house burglaries. In other words, you need to develop news angles through which to connect to the daily and weekly news agenda.

It might also mean developing different sets of messages and facts to promote in your news and feature output in order to give a regional or local immediacy to a national campaign. Thus, many media relations strategies and campaigns are underpinned by freshly commissioned *research* which offers a client ownership of an issue and 'expert' positioning.

Finally, timing is everything in media relations. How and when will you release the information to create maximum impact and integrate this dimension of the overall PR and marketing with other elements of the promotion?

EXERCISE:

Using some of the pointers above, can you outline the media relations strategy of one of your key clients?

Can you articulate the strategy in three or four bullet points which summarise the plan?

Building the media toolkit

If you are putting together a media relations programme for a client, there are certain building blocks, or collateral, which you are going to need in order to satisfy the journalist's agenda. These need not be complex necessarily, but they must reflect the information policy and wider communications objectives of the client and present useful information for press in the most user friendly way possible.

What might this media toolkit look like, for example, for a company entering the media relations arena for the first time? It could include some, or all of the following:

Factpack: Series of backgrounders covering key aspects of the company: size, turnover, offices, markets, etc.

FAQ: Frequently Asked Questions, which pre-empt typical journalist queries on key parts of the company's activity.

Positioning Statements: Covering the company's view on issues at the top of the industry's agenda.

People profiles: Potted biographies of the company's key people, most especially the spokespeople and their areas of expertise.

Image bank: Colour and black and white images, usually digital these days, which illustrate in an imaginative way the company and its people at work. These images could be available for download from the company website, or from Flickr, and perhaps extended to video clips accessed through YouTube.

News releases: An archive of available news releases going back at least a year or so, which give a very good take on all recent major announcements and initiatives.

Online media channels

Everyone is online these days. People of all ages and stages now read daily news and features online; in fact, the business model underpinning newspapers in hard copy has never looked shakier. It is therefore no coincidence that every daily newspaper in the country has an online version, which is now the principal hub for every aspect of the publishing operation, with the actual print version of the newspaper reduced to just one, albeit important, component part.

When you examine news, features and comment more closely on the web, you can discern a subtle shift in the pattern of what works well. It is this pattern you need to isolate and reproduce, because reading material comfortably on the web requires a different approach to the printed page.

You are aiming for copy that is easy to access, easy to read, modular, active and simple, though not dumbed down. If you want great examples of news and feature writing on the web, go to the BBC website (www.bbc.co.uk).

Basic rules for online copy :

1. Use single decker headlines, with subject, object & active verb
2. Maximum of two sentences per paragraph, no more than 16 words per sentence. (Makes it easy to read!)
3. Space between every paragraph

4. Simple language, but not dumbed down – no long words!
5. No more than 350 words per story, so that the attention span doesn't get over stretched
6. Imaginative use of graphics, pictures and captions
7. Loads of quotes to make it live

Guide to common digital media outputs

Blogs: A short form for weblog, sometimes defined as a frequent and chronological publication of comments and thoughts on the web. Blogs usually include philosophical reflections, opinions on the Internet and social or political issues. In effect, a blog is information that is instantly published to a website where users post informal journals of their thoughts, comments, and philosophies, updated frequently and normally reflecting the views of the blog's creator. Bloggers have become highly influential in shaping opinion and as a source of expert comment on products, services and issues.

Twitter: A foreshortened, 140-character format that lets anyone upload to the web anything from an observation about the state of the traffic to a major news headline. Increasingly in today's media relations landscape Twitter has become an important channel through which to release news to the media, and to generate a following of journalists who have a declared interest in your news.

RSS Feeds: 'Really Simple Syndication', or RSS, is a method of moving the news model from 'push' to 'pull'. Journalists and others interested in your organisation can subscribe to your RSS Feed which automatically delivers news output onto their PC or mobile phone. This format is incredibly useful for creating communities of interest who want to listen to what you have to say.

SMS Text Messaging: Another very powerful mechanism for getting simple, clear messages across to a wide variety of audiences, from consumers to specialists, and a channel increasingly used by PR teams when disseminating information.

MNRs: Multimedia News Releases (MNRs), sometimes called social media news releases, enable you to create three-dimensional news output, comprising a mix of words, video, still images, short chunks of copy and hyperlinks. This new and developing format allows your news and information to go wider and deeper, playing across all the digital platforms, either through hosting on an intermediary site or your own.

Pitching to journalists

Like going on stage to act or play an instrument, the last link in the learning chain is going 'live' with something. Pitching a story is the final link in the media relations chain and it is a part of the job that even some senior PRs will run a mile from if they have a chance. For some reason, picking up a phone to, or getting face-to-face with, a real live journalist is not something that many people find easy, quite the opposite in fact.

Many journalists are less intimidating than they might seem, but to find their cuddlier side, the trick is to get to them at the right moment with an idea presented in the right format, at speed. This means doing a lot of homework on your story or feature idea before you pick up the phone. Be sure when the question 'What is the story?' is asked, that you have an answer. Anticipate questions and have further answers ready. Understand the strength of the story you are offering or the attraction of the features package you are putting together.

Broadly speaking there are a range of bases you need to cover if you are going to increase your hit rate:

- Know the title you are pitching to: if you haven't even read the publication, don't know what the journalist has been covering or don't have a grasp of the readership, you are likely to fall at the first hurdle, so do some basic homework before your approach.
- Build relationships face-to-face where possible: there is everything to be gained and nothing to lose by making contact with a journalist and buying them a cup of coffee or a quick lunch to establish where your mutual interests lie. Like every other walk of life, success is sometimes about who you know and building personal trust. Remember the maxim: 'good media relations means good relations with the media'.
- Have a story or a few feature ideas ready when you speak to or meet up with a journo. If you don't, it will be a missed opportunity and they are less likely

to see you as a fertile source for copy in the future. Follow these verbal pitches and ideas up via a prompt email to get them locked in.

- Focus on putting together timely and interesting feature packages that contain:
  - a news hook;
  - a good, articulate spokesperson;
  - a relevant case study;
  - access to images which are powerful and complement your story.

This means setting aside some time to really understand how features work and what journalists need.

- Develop an understanding of how each journalist likes to be pitched to. Is it phone call, follow-up email and then second phone call, or is just an email with the headline in the title bar? Or maybe an opening pitch idea on the phone, followed by a meeting?

CHAPTER SIX

Working the News Agenda

Introduction; PR & the news interface; what is news?; news release triggers; mastering the form; tailoring news; uses for the news release; news management process; best practice; news writing exercises;

Introduction

If media relations is still the bread and butter of most PR campaigns, then the news release remains the workhorse of most media relations programmes. This tried and tested way of generating column inches is still the first port of call for the PRO intent on winning coverage for his or her clients. Create the story, put it in a release, then put it out there and score some quick wins. Or so the orthodoxy goes.

What's more, the orthodoxy has history behind it. The first recorded news release was issued as long ago as 1906, by Ivy Ledbetter Lee. An ex-journalist on the New York Times, Lee was the public relations counsel to the Pennsylvania Railroad Company. A fatal crash involving one of its trains in Atlantic City had taken place and Lee wanted to give journalists the facts as the company saw them before any misreporting could undermine the reputation of the company. He persuaded the management to let him issue a pre-emptive 'press release' to head off any negative publicity. He went even further, organising a train for journalists to visit the site of the crash and see for themselves. This press release was to be the first of many issued by Lee on behalf of his corporate clients. Initially regarded by journalists with great suspicion, these releases soon gained traction and became the front-line weapon in Lee's media armoury.

But do news releases still deliver the goods, or have they been superceded by tweets, blogs and media 'advisories'? Are they still as effective as general perceptions would like them to be? The fact is that many news releases don't make it very far through the most basic selection process. They are quickly screened out and spiked by a news sub-editor after scanning the headline and first paragraph. All that hard work gone to waste. All those client expectations to manage!

The ones that succeed do so because they conform to the demands of the news story genre. They meet simple, but clear criteria that qualify them as news. The content, the timing and the pitch, or angle, come together to tell a compelling story, one that is topical, interesting and relevant to the audience, one that demands to be on a news page because we need to know about it.

Sniffing out a story and turning it into a successful news release is something that can improve with practice. In that sense there is no magic formula to learn, but rather a proven methodology to follow. Working PR consultants need to increase their hit rate and score more consistent successes with news releases. Part of doing that is a mindset – when you are looking for and thinking 'news', you will see it everywhere. The other part is giving yourself the practical tools to do the job. When the two come together, you are a more effective and more convincing PR operator.

The PR and news interface

PR practitioners and journalists often work closely together in the news arena. This is because journalists rely on sources for much of their information and access to these sources is often provided by press officers and PR teams. As gatekeepers to the news content and distribution mechanism, PRs often control the news flow.

For the PR professional, learning how to ride and sometimes shape the news agenda is critical to positioning the client commercially, communicating key messages about the company and its culture and, perhaps most importantly, connecting it to issues that are central in the public mind. Put another way, if you are not part of the news agenda you are not at the front of peoples' minds and therefore, by definition, the space you have left is likely to be filled by a competitor.

A study commissioned by *The Guardian*'s Nick Davies to coincide with his book *Flat Earth News,*★ revealed some telling statistics which, taken together, suggest that PR professionals who know what they are doing are very successful

★ *Flat Earth News*, Nick Davies, Chatto, Feb 2008

at dominating the news content of our quality newspapers. Davies calls this content 'churnulism'.

For example, the study by Cardiff University School of Journalism showed:

- 12% of stories in British newspapers consist of a story that a reporter has found out and pursued on his/her own initiative.
- 60% of quality-print stories consist wholly or in part of wire copy and/or PR material.
- 20% of quality-print stories contain clear elements of PR-driven material.
- 8% of stories are unable to be sourced accurately.
- 30% of home news stories are direct rewrites of Press Association and other news agency copy.
- 19% are 'largely reproduced' from this copy

Amongst other observations, Davies also points out that, for the first time, there are now more PR practitioners in the UK than journalists. It all goes to prove one thing, that PR people who know what they are doing have every chance of getting their news picked up by most news outlets, many of them struggling with fewer staff and resources and thus less able to spend time and effort generating original content.

What is news?

"News is any overt act which juts out of the routine of circumstance. A good public relations man advises his client…to carry out an overt act…interrupting the continuity of life in some way to bring about a response." So said Edward Bernays, the founder of modern public relations practice, in conversation with American author Stewart Ewen, writer of *'Captains of Consciousness'*.

In general, news is new information, of universal interest. It has a strong, time-definite context and a rationale which often accommodates rapid change and an unfolding scenario. News stories are often dramas in themselves, but they are always high impact, instant and compelling stories which add to our knowledge about the people and world that directly affects us. Within the news genre there are different types of news and the ability to distinguish between them is critical:

- 'Hard' news tends to be reflected in TV and radio bulletins, daily newspapers and online media. It is instant, 'universal', and exists in a state of perpetual motion. Hard news stories develop through the hour, and through the day – the Iraq War, a General Election, a financial scandal, the credit crunch and so on. Hard news happens 24/7.

- 'Soft' news is less time-definite, less critical and more disposable. It can be a human interest story, a new trend identified by researchers, or something a person has said about someone else. Whilst it is important, it can wait.
- 'Specialist' news is particular to an industry or interest group. It accommodates, for example, many business related stories printed in trade and vertical sector press – information that is interesting in its context, but which has little popular appeal beyond its immediate audience.
- A photo-story is simply a news story told in pictures – either through film or video, or a still photograph. With a photo-story, it is the picture that does the work; the words are there to reinforce, by providing detail via a 'caption' or commentary. This genre of news can be explosive in its impact and illustrative of an issue for many years to come; just think of the iconic images associated with news coverage of the Vietnam war, Hurricane Katrina or the London Olympics.
- A 'filler' is a term used to describe a piece of news which is inconsequential but about which people want to know. Examples of fillers might be news that an actress has started a new relationship, is sporting a new hairstyle or has gone on a crash diet. This 'news' increasingly clogs up the airwaves and the pages of newspapers, magazines and websites. It is a vehicle full of possibilities for the PR practitioner to exploit.

One of the most important ways in which PR practitioners need to develop their skills is to become professional consumers of news. It is not good enough to simply read a daily newspaper as a passive bystander; we need to understand what type of news it is that we are reading and isolate the reasons why it works as a story. At the same time, we will begin to recognise the provenance of individual news stories and the news values that have made them work. Through this process, we are on the road to becoming more effective manipulators of the news agenda.

News release triggers

In order to commoditise news, or at least inject some process into its treatment, it can be helpful to use the concept of news *'triggers',* In this sense, a trigger is used to denote important developments which tend, by their nature, to repeat. Thus, if you are planning and managing news output and looking for stories to develop, you will know that the signing of a significant new contract for a company is fertile ground for a news release, as experience tells us the story is highly likely to be used by the business pages of target press, especially if you can put a figure on the value of the contract.

What are the most common news release triggers that most Business To Business (B2B) or consumer (B2C) PRs face in a typical week? Where can you look for news opportunities and angles, and where do they generally come from? Some suggestions might include:

B2B (Business):

- Contract wins (with a financial number)
- Product launches
- Events (major events such as AGMs, conferences etc)
- Major corporate announcements (restructure/merger/expansion/redundancy)
- Strategic alliances
- Appointments (senior ones)
- Financial results.

B2C (Consumer):

- New products and services
- New research: behaviour, attitudes, perceptions, trends
- Issues: health; education; housing; personal finance
- The impact of new legislation
- Human interest, people!
- Quirky happenings
- Picture stories

- Which of these news opportunities have you identified and taken in the last six months?
- What other opportunities can you identify and add to the list?

You want to maximise your chances of attracting the news editor's attention with your news release. That means writing it in a certain way which shows that you know the rules and which doesn't act as a turn-off.

News stories are top-down constructs; they seek to give the maximum amount of information as quickly as possible, answering the questions: 'What; Who; Why; When; and Where (known as the five 'W's) – and 'How'? This is so because sub-editors cut from the bottom up to meet changing demands for space. In the world of news, everyone has limited time and limited patience. Make their job easier and you get one step nearer you goal. Classic news stories (and hence news releases) tend to follow the same, proven structure:

FIGURE 1: CLASSICAL NEWS STORY STRUCTURE :

Headline:	One short sentence carried over two lines max: subject; object; active verb: 'MAN BITES DOG IN SUPERMARKET SHOCK'
News point: WWW	In a vicious attack at JD Supermarket this morning, 55-year-old Dave Stewart bit a Golden Retriever in the leg.
News point (2) – Reinforcing WWH	The dog, three-year-old Jessie, was not badly injured, but Mr Stewart is now undergoing extensive psychological tests in hospital.
Context	This is the third such attack in as many months and is the source of growing worry amongst health authorities and the police.
Quote – brings story to life	"I've never seen anything like it. He came at Jessie out of nowhere. It was very distressing," said Jessie's owner, Bob Sturgess.
Exposition, detail	Mr Stewart's neighbour, Alan Little, said he had observed worrying changes in his friend's behaviour over preceding weeks, revealing that Mr Stewart had recently moved into a kennel in his garden.

Exposition, second quote	Said local Police Chief, Norman McTaggart: "We are asking shoppers and the wider public to be vigilant while we try and establish a link between these incidents."
Expert Comment, Balance	Psychologist Martin Mindreader, an acknowledged expert in human behaviour, claimed that this type of attack might be due to growing stress levels causing certain character types to regress to an animal state.

Mastering the form

As already suggested, to maximise your chances of success it is helpful to follow the technical rules of news release writing and master the form as well as content. Observing the rules shows you know what you are doing, and does not provide the excuse for an impatient sub-editor to turn off your story just because it doesn't meet a technical benchmark. Here is a good practical guideline to ensure your release conforms but, if in any doubt, you should follow the design template used within your own team.

FIGURE 2: CLASSICAL NEWS STORY FORM:

Headline	**BOLD/UPPER CASE:** MAN BITES DOG IN SUPERMARKET SHOCK
Qualifying Sub-Head	**BOLD/UPPER & LOWER CASE:** -Retriever Escapes With Minor Injuries-
Date at start of first para	**BOLD/UPPER & LOWER CASE** 1st December 2012
Add place of issue to make *dateline* (usually Head Office)	London, 1st December 2012
One & a half line spacing throughout	This leaves room for on-the-page changes carried out by sub-editors
Divide into short paras	Story should comprise a number of paras constructed around content – pyramid structure determines order, with most important at top

Contact details at end	**BOLD/UPPER LOWER CASE** For further information, please contact:
Notes To Editors	After contact details, *Notes To Editors* should contain, in single line spacing, additional information still relevant to that in body of the release. The boilerplate (company descriptor) also goes here.
Overall length	Two A4 pages, with Notes To Editors, two pages max.
Reference	Reference source at bottom so you can trace the story on your system.

Tailoring news

Embedding key messages, quotes

The principal PR purpose behind drafting and distributing news releases is to tell your audiences what your organisation is doing. But it is also an opportunity to get across a key message that you want your audience to remember about you. The best place to embed this key message is in the quote that you ascribe to your spokesperson who is flagged in the news release. A good tip with quotes is that they only really work if you can hear the spokesperson actually delivering the line; authenticity is all about speaking words that resonate. Too many PR-driven quotes are simply not authentic, often being too complex, too full of jargon and too long.

Example of a 'good' quote:

"This new model combines the latest technology with a host of features to offer users a faster, more efficient and affordable experience," said John Doe Laptops Ltd CEO, Tom Draper.

Finding news angles

Your 'news angle' is a term that is sometimes misunderstood but which means, in essence, the skill of associating your news story with a topical, or current issue that is already on the news agenda, for example, a new car that runs on hydrogen making a contribution to the cutting of carbon emissions on the roads, or a new type of home security lock helping to reduce rising neighbourhood crime. Finding a news angle is a skill you develop with time, but the ability to find these angles becomes a real differentiator between those who can manipulate the news agenda well or not.

Boilerplates

The boilerplate is a standard wording that describes your organisation and its principal features; perhaps products, staff numbers, office locations and stock market ticker reference (if you are a quoted company). A boilerplate is usually no longer than two sentences and is attached to every news release that goes out.

Using pictures

Illustrations are often overlooked by PR practitioners, but any journalist will confirm that a news release accompanied by a high-quality image massively increases the chances of take-up. Alongside photography, images also include charts, graphs, cartoons and screen grabs from websites.

Grammar and punctuation

It is part of the PR professional's job to make sure that all copy released conforms to house style, uses accurate grammar and is spellchecked and fact checked for accuracy. Remember that the credibility of your client's information partly rests on its presentation, and thus a mix of form and content.

Uses for the news release

News releases certainly are workhorses; they are versatile and adaptable to a variety of media relations situations. Consider the following:

- General news story: A 'top line' story written for and distributed to principal target news media;
- Specialist news stories: A series of stories 'sliced and diced' to meet more

specialist needs; for example, where you might carve up a large survey into a variety of stories according to vertical or geographical sector interest. Many business stories also fit this category;

- A feature: News stories are often used as the starting point for a more extended news feature, perhaps in conjunction with a backgrounder. Features editors and writers often find their stories this way;

- Press conferences: If you have decided to have a press conference – and the decision will hang on the quality of the news values you are looking at – then the news release will underpin what is said at the event and form the basis of the story that journalists will take away and write.

- Media briefings: Often your news release will be used by a spokesperson as a source of information, or focus, for a face-to-face or down-the-line interview with a journalist. Because journalists need more than colour, or background, the news release is helpful to bring them back to the story.

- Events: news releases can be written to highlight events which, though uncontroversial, might still be interesting to the media, for example anniversaries or company milestones.

- Blogs and tweets: Used as starting points for a range of social media communications, certainly by bloggers and users of Twitter feeds, but also LinkedIn and Facebook.

- RSS Feeds: Really Simple Syndication (RSS) enables journalists and others to 'pull' your news releases directly onto their mobile devices.

News management process

The flow of information in and out of a company, or corporate communications department, is usually highly controlled and a direct function of *information policy*. It is the business of policy makers to establish precisely what it is a company will, or will not, talk about and why. In the same way, larger organisations will develop criteria for what is and isn't news and an associated process for managing it.

Information is often commercially sensitive, the more so where a company has a quoted share price or complex strategic alliances with partners. Inaccurate information, or information sent out at the wrong time, can have a very damaging effect on a business – quickly spreading negative impact via the web to shareholders, staff and clients. Likewise, senior executives in a company need to be very careful about comment they might make or opinion they might express on competitors or issues which impact their position in the market or share price.

Before they are written and distributed, news releases should have to go through a news management and approvals process. It is your responsibility to conform to this approvals process or, if one is not in place, to work with the client to ensure that a suitable mechanism is set up. Make sure you and your team know and observe the approvals process for each and every client.

FIGURE 1: TYPICAL NEWS MANAGEMENT PROCESS:

PROCESS	APPROVAL
Subject conforms to company news criteria: the starting gate of the process	PRO
If subject conforms, then produce first draft of news release	PRO Client
Second draft including corrections	PRO Client
Final draft, sign-offs	Possible legal, HR department involvement if subject is controversial Released on approved signature from nominated signatories
*Q&A: Managing objections and questions related to the story	PRO Legal
Distribution: compile media list & agree timing	PRO

Ten Tips To Improve Your Chances!

• Make sure your subject has high news values. Try to give it a sense of immediacy. Use words like 'today announced'. If it has no real news values, don't release it.

*Q&As are optional depending on the importance and sensitivity of the story

- Use news release paper, or write 'news release' at the top of the first page which should be on letterhead paper.
- Present the essential facts immediately in the first paragraph, especially the 'who' and 'what'. Always write your release so that it makes sense if the editor is short of space and deletes paragraphs from the bottom up.
- Use a punchy, factual, eye-catching headline. News editors skim read 50 or 60 stories a minute, so your story must grab attention immediately.
- Adopt a simple, plain language style. Avoid jargon, and ensure the information is easy to understand. Clarity is a must. Fancy, pretentious writing will obscure your message and reduce your chances of gaining coverage.
- Keep your release concise, informative and interesting. Use one and a half or double line spacing. Do not go to more than two pages.
- Keep each paragraph tight, with no more than four short sentences.
- Put the date at the top of the release so news editors know that the story is still current.
- Leave adequate space at the top and in the margins for the sub-editor to make any changes.
- Do not underline words. This is an instruction for journalists to use italics.

Other points to remember!

- Language should be easy to understand: words short, paras short, one idea per sentence.
- Spokespeople quoted in past tense.
- For local media, your story should always have a local angle.
- Human interest stories or unusual angles interest the media.
- Journalists are not paid to use the material you supply.
- You cannot dictate how much of the copy will be used or when it will appear.
- The amount of space or air time a publication or radio station gives you is *their* editorial decision.
- You are not entitled to see the finished copy!

Best practice

If you are looking for examples of best practice in news release writing, a usually reliable source is provided by the press offices of government departments. They will usually follow a formula which is technically correct and designed to do the best job, simply, in a way that engages journalists highly effectively. Check this out for yourself, but see the example below:

New business bank to support up to £10 billion of business lending

- **24 September 2012 10:00**

Department for Business, Innovation and Skills

BIS | Department for Business
Innovation & Skills

- **Business Secretary Vince Cable will announce today (24 September) the first steps in creating a Government-backed business bank, including new Government funding of £1 billion.**
- It will aim to attract private sector funding so that when fully operational, it could support up to £10 billion of new and additional business lending.

The Government will build a single institution that will address long-standing, structural gaps in the supply of finance, identified in Tim Breedon's report on non-bank finance. It will bring together in one place Government finance support for small and mid-sized businesses. It will also control the Government's interests in a new wholesale funding mechanism which will be developed to unlock institutional investment to benefit small businesses.

Vince Cable said: "For decades British industry has lacked the sort of diverse, long-term finance that is quite normal elsewhere. We need a British business bank with a clean balance sheet and a mandate to expand lending rapidly and we are now going to get it.

"Alongside the private sector, the bank will get the market lending to manufacturers, exporters and growth companies that so desperately need support. It will be a lasting monument to our determination to reshape finance so it can finally serve industry the way it should. Its success will not be the scale of its own direct interventions but how far it shakes up the market in business finance and helps to ease constraints for high-growth firms.

"Having a functioning, diverse supply of finance is an integral part of the Government's industrial strategy. It is all about making the right decisions now to secure our long-term industrial success."

The bank will operate at arms-length from Government. It will be professionally run and commercially focused. It will facilitate the provision of loans, including long-term capital, to UK firms through banks and other financial institutions. By harnessing the power of capital markets, it has the potential to transform business finance in the UK.

The new institution will operate through the wholesale markets, it will not have any retail presence and will not displace or subsidise banks. Its role is to encourage the development of private sector solutions and enable the market to work properly, not compete with it.

More detail on the design of the bank and the types of interventions it will support will be provided in the autumn.

Notes to Editors

1. Proposals to widen business access to new and alternative sources of finance were published by the independent taskforce on non-bank lending in March 2012. The taskforce, chaired by Tim Breedon, CEO of Legal & General plc, was commissioned by the Government to examine a range of alternative and sustainable finance sources, particularly for small and medium-sized enterprises (SMEs). The report, *Boosting finance options for business*, can be downloaded from **here**.

2. The Government's economic policy objective is to achieve 'strong, sustainable and balanced growth that is more evenly shared across the country and between industries.' It set four ambitions in the *'Plan for Growth'* *(PDF 1.7MB)*, published at Budget 2011:
   - To create the most competitive tax system in the G20
   - To make the UK the best place in Europe to start, finance and grow a business
   - To encourage investment and exports as a route to a more balanced economy
   - To create a more educated workforce that is the most flexible in Europe.

   Work is underway across Government to achieve these ambitions, including progress on more than 250 measures as part of the Growth Review. Developing an Industrial Strategy gives new impetus to this work by providing businesses, investors and the public with more clarity about the long-term direction in which the Government wants the economy to travel.

3. BIS's online newsroom contains the latest press notices and speeches, as well as video and images for download. It also features an up to date list of BIS press office contacts. See http://www.bis.gov.uk/newsroom for more information.

Contact Information

Name BIS Press Office
Job Title
Division Department for Business, Innovation & Skills
Phone
Fax
Mobile
Email bispress.releases@bis.gsi.gov.uk

NEWS WRITING EXERCISES

Below is a brief put out by Jetpak Corporation* promoting its new jet powered backpack to be used by the emergency services to speed up incident response rates and help fight crime at the same time. The brief is supported by a few facts that provide context for the development.

Looking at this as a media relations exercise, we want to work out how many news releases we can construct and for which audiences. At the same time, we want to work out what angles we should develop to make these news releases topical and directly relevant to the selected audience.

Read the brief carefully. Note the detail and the context. Now assume that we want to send out the news releases today, targeted in the following ways and using the angles we have developed in the boxes below. Also note the fact that we have identified a precise journalist and publication to receive each release because it helps us to focus the content more clearly.

Release One:
Audience: Consumers
Media target: National newspapers
Sample correspondent: Home affairs correspondent, The Times
Angle: Helping the fight against crime in inner city areas

---

*Jetpak Corporation is a fictitious organisation

Release Two:
Audience: Procurement departments, emergency services
Media target: Vertical sector press
Sample correspondent: Editor, Police Review
Angle: This equipment will help meet rapid response targets

Release Three:
Audience: High Net Worth Individuals (HNWI)
Media Target: HNWI Media
Sample correspondent: News editor, How To Spend It
Angle: Exclusive travel accessory

Now see if you can write the headline, newspoints (WWWWWH), find an appropriate context and draft a quote with a key message. See how your headline and story change subtly as you exploit each different angle.

Check your versions against the ones you can find in Chapter Thirteen.

JETPAK CORPORATION
LAUNCH BRIEF

Background

Jetpak Corporation is a joint venture between: Jetpak Inc, a private company based in Houston, Texas; the North American Space Agency (NASA); and the US Government. The company has been working for a number of years to perfect a commercial prototype for a personal vehicle using rocket technology for use in military and civilian emergency situations. The strategy behind development of a device of this kind would be the speed, manoeuvrability and functionality that it would bring to rapid response situations, such as incidents of crime and health-related emergency.

Having completed and deployed a military version (JP1 'The HitMan'), Jetpak Inc. has now developed and licensed a version for civilian uses (JP2 'Mercury'). This is in the form of a large, but lightweight pack that is strapped onto the back of the user, employing rocket fuel propulsion and finger controlled navigation systems to ascend, descend and traverse with great speed and precision. Mercury is the ultimate single-user, rapid response mechanism in the world, with a working range of 35 miles and total flight time of two hours.

In Q3 last year, Jetpak Corporation obtained the appropriate licenses from the UK Government to approach the emergency services – fire, police and ambulance – to begin testing the Mercury model for use in the UK. With testing complete, the company now wishes to launch Mercury across the UK to all the regional police, fire and ambulance services and sell 250 units this year. It also wishes to target consumers to let them know that this technology will be making a massive difference to saving lives and making communities safer places to be, particularly inner urban areas with high incidences of violent crime.

Mercury is very expensive, with individual models costing £150,000, including a training programme, pilot qualification and back-up. The license acquired from the government enables users to fly at heights of up to 100 metres. Whilst it is not a primary audience, the company also wishes to target High Net Worth Individuals (HNWIs) to develop a private market for Mercury. It sees possibilities for a premium pricing focused on an exclusive quality brand based around an international club of users. There is currently no regulation in force banning private use of these vehicles. This market is important to the company and is intrinsic to its vision of launch success.

Jetpak wants to launch now, with a high impact, maximum sizzle campaign. It has allocated a working budget of £500,000 to cover this activity and is prepared to field an impressive array of spokespeople to front the product, including scientists, military and police users.

JETPAK FAST FACTS

- Home Office crime statistics show a small reduction in violent crime overall in the UK last year, but with a 4% increase in violent crime in inner city areas.
- The ambulance service has submitted a formal complaint to the Home Office asking them to remove 'sleeping policemen' from many inner city roads, as they slow down vehicle speeds.
- Emergency services response times are failing to meet targets by an average of 8% across the three emergency services, with ambulance service times least efficient of the three, at 11%.
- Some ambulance service crews are refusing to enter a small number of

blacklisted housing estates where they claim to be in fear for their own safety. These estates are in the cities of Liverpool, Manchester, Rochdale, Hull and London, to name a few.

- On-the-spot treatment of the right kind by qualified staff will offer trauma injury victims a 33% improved chance of survival, according to a recent study in the *British Medical Journal*.
- Fire service statistics show that improved access for appliances and crews could be a life saver in a limited number of high density urban areas.

CHAPTER SEVEN

Wider and Deeper with Features

Features & how they work: differentiating news & features; definitions & categories; the classic feature types; feature construction; the feature body; intros & outros; how PR features work; style & impact;

Features and how they work

Feature writing, along with reporting and writing news stories, is part of the bread and butter of being a working journalist. All journalists who have been formally trained have been taught how to research and write a feature.

Whilst the same is true of the PR's job, it is not always true of the training, much of which is done in a more opportunistic and less methodical way. Thus many PRs tend to feel less comfortable with a feature assignment, often unsure about how to develop, pitch and execute an idea that will deliver the right balance between the interests of the client and the chosen publication and, most importantly of all, hold the attention of the reader.

Mastering this form of editorial output has tremendous possibilities for PROs, simply because feature length coverage in target press affords the opportunity to generate coverage of people, organisations and issues that goes both wider and deeper than news. It is through written and broadcast features that we can generate the most editorial exposure, so these should be an intrinsic part of our media relations programmes.

Of course, like most things in life, feature writing improves with practice. So remember that the basics are just that. The rest depends on a lot of hard work and a little inspiration.

Differentiating news and features

News writing	Feature writing
The five Ws: Who, what, why, where, when	Develops the related issue
Factual	Opinion and depth
Black and White	Colour
Need to know	Want to know
Past tense	Present tense

Use journalistic writing techniques

GOOD	BAD
Short words	Long-winded/unfamiliar words
Short sentences	Complex sentences
Short paragraphs	Rambling paragraphs
Active language	Passive voice
Plain English	Jargon and technobabble

Definitions and categories

Like most other craft skills, the characteristics and dynamics of features become clearer when you inject some process into your approach. Features tend to be what we read when we have digested the news. They are usually topical, derived from a current issue or developed from yesterday's headline. In any case, the word 'feature' implies a showcase to develop an idea which is compelling and informative for the reader. Not only that, but a feature should be written in a way that can entertain, enlighten and even surprise as well. Writing a good feature takes more skill and is more of a pressure than writing a good news story.

Every substantial publication and broadcast outlet runs features. Why? Because they are a staple of the media diet and expected by readers and viewers. They give us access to insights, information, background and personalities that we didn't know about. Whilst feature stories can contain in-depth analysis, opinion and polemic, they are neither *columns* nor *leaders,* which both perform specific but separate functions. Features are news, issues and personality driven. Whether highbrow or lowbrow, business or consumer, we all read features because that is where so much of our information – and thus our conversation – comes from.

The feature assumes many guises. It may be a profile of a person or a group: an athlete in Team GB; a singer such as Adele; a politician or political organisation; a team – a football club; or an army unit in Helmand Province. Or perhaps it is an in-depth look at a social issue, like violence in schools, stressed out NHS staff or eating disorders; in a business context, it could include subjects as diverse as corporate governance and the bank lending crisis or the impact of computer viruses. If you can think of it, you can probably write a feature about it.

A feature is usually longer than a news story, but beyond a point length in itself is not a requirement. What's more important is the form the story takes. Think of the feature as the journalistic equivalent of an essay which often explores several points of view, even when it is focused on one individual. Remember too, that features do not appear exclusively on the printed page; both radio and television depend on features to widen and deepen their coverage of people and issues.

In feature writing it can be useful to view the task in the same way that you might tell a story. Although not a classic dramatic story, a feature must be on the way somewhere, it cannot simply move around aimlessly in concentric circles. The reader needs to be taken on a journey through an issue or around a personality in a way that is directed and focused; there must be a beginning, a middle and an end to the journey. The more you break them down, the more you realise that the best stories work in a particular way; they have a structure that accommodates certain fixed points on the trajectory.

The master of the structure of dramatic story telling, albeit in the context of film, is Robert McKee. In his seminal book 'Story'* he deconstructs the way in which the most compelling stories work and suggests there is a process that invariably lends itself to successful drama. He starts with the notion that every story must have a controlling idea driving it, a theory or supposition which the piece then sets out to test as it moves along its trajectory.

McKee suggests that the 'classic' dramatic story has five key elements in its structure. Without all of these elements the story cannot progress or resolve in

*Story, Robert McKee, Methuen, 1998

a way in which ultimately satisfies the reader (or in his case the viewer). These five stages comprise:

- The inciting incident: an event which is the primary cause of all that follows.
- Progressive complications: nothing moves forward without conflict; something must be at stake.
- The crisis: the ultimate decision has to be taken from which there is no turning back.
- The climax: the crowning major reversal, when the protagonist is tested to the limit and found not to be wanting.
- Resolution: the final phase deals with any remaining material or issues that follow the climax.

Whilst not suggesting that feature writing replicates dramatic storytelling necessarily, or proposing there is a formulaic approach that presents a panacea to the aspiring feature writer, it is worth learning some of the craft skills which govern this most creative and satisfying aspect of media relations.

The classic feature types

To carry forward the idea of process and craft a little further, when we know what we are looking for we can divide features into quite easily recognisable types. With variations, these recur across most media most of the time:

The news feature

A news story tells the audience what happened. A news feature will tell them why and how it happened, how the people involved are reacting, and what impact the decision is having on other people. News features tend to appear in the wake of breaking news stories, or even alongside them. Today's news story gives us the result of the General Election, tomorrow's news feature tells us where the election was won and lost and what the new government might do in its first 100 days.

The cover feature

Cover features are usually in-depth treatments of an important subject, perhaps an issue, emerging trend or major event, based on original research and extensive reporting. A magazine will often sell an issue on the basis of an exclusive cover feature of compelling interest to its readers. Generally, this form of the medium is longer and may employ box stories and deep picture captions to explore subplots and parallel themes to the main story. For example, a three-page spread on the many different facets of the war in Afghanistan at any given moment.

The personality in profile

Generate coverage for your clients with a profile of an interesting person or organisation. You can look at someone who's making news in your business, in the community or in almost any form of human endeavour. There is little that interests readers more than other people, whether prominent or unsung. They are an endless source of fascination and human engagement. To see how it is done, look out for profiles of individuals who, for example, have just written a book, launched a stand-up comedy tour or are about to debut in a West End play.

The case study or application

Case studies are most often used to illustrate what happened when a company or person met a specific business challenge and overcame it. Hence they often appear in a curtailed format, sometimes centred on a standardised series of headings: '*Challenge, Solution and Benefits*'. The case study sets out to provide a record of the 'real life' solution to a problem, achieved with the help of a particular product or service, and the subsequent benefits it delivers. Case studies can be long and complex or short and sweet and they hold endless possibilities for PROs.

The picture feature

As the title suggests, picture features, or spreads, tell a more extended story of an event principally by using pictures rather than words. Picture features are one of the most instantly accessible and compelling ways of telling an extended story and have themselves spawned a separate industry via magazines such as *Heat, OK!* And *Hello*. However, tabloid newspapers and current affairs magazines will often run picture features as a double page spread.

Research survey and trends

This feature type typically takes as its jumping off point new statistics and findings about a particular topic or issue that has popular appeal. It might be, for example, the latest British Crime Survey Report on whether crime in general, and specific crimes in particular, like violent crime, have risen or fallen and why. What are the stories, human and otherwise, behind the figures? How is violent crime impacting on your town and your neighbours?

The historical, or milestone feature

The trigger for this feature type is usually an anniversary or a specific milestone which can be used as a jumping-off point for a wider look at an issue or an organisation in the context of time having passed. For example, take the 60th anniversary of the D-Day landings in Normandy. What has happened to the veterans who took part? How have the French come to terms with the destruction and rebuilt their towns? How can society stop such carnage from happening again?

The 'How To' or DIY feature

This usually is developed from an idea that can be adapted for wider consumption. The popular appeal lies in taking a basic idea and applying it to a personal context. For example, a celebrity chef comes up with some recipes and ideas on healthy eating. How can they be translated for use by people like us – busy singles, working mothers with school age children – people who need to produce good, healthy and nutritious food quickly, but who cannot follow time consuming ideas or afford expensive ingredients? One classic approach to the 'how to' feature is to divide the information into 10 steps, or 10 top tips. For example: 'The 10-step plan to buying property overseas'.

The 'soft' feature or 'filler'

Usually based on a slight idea, soft features combine words and pictures around any topical piece of gossip or news which can be built into a more general perspective. Soft features can be found in all consumer facing magazines, for example 'Steal Her Style' in *Heat Magazine*, or 'Houses of the Week' in the 'Home' Section of the *Sunday Times*.

Try the following tips for locating feature ideas amongst your client portfolio:

- A new product or service that might have the potential to change behaviours or processes. What would that newly changed world look like? Who could you speak to, apart from the client, that might be able to paint a picture for you?
- A powerful or iconoclastic individual has views which are controversial and interesting. Where do they fit in the wider scheme of things and how would they benefit from contrasting with others, perhaps equally powerful? What do they have to say that is provocative, exciting or new?
- A survey that throws up newsworthy trends, patterns or behaviours also releases the potential for further investigation. For example, a survey that shows one in four people do not consider fiddling an insurance claim to be fraud, has all sorts of interesting possibilities. Why not? What has happened to our notion of morality? Is this kind of behaviour duplicated elsewhere and what do various constituencies think about it?
- A news story or development is reported in the mainstream press that your client may be able to say something intelligent and interesting about. Say for example that the hospitality industry reports that the SARS virus has stopped business travel stone dead and people are videoconferencing instead. If this is what your client does it is a golden opportunity to put an opportunistic feature together that shows the client, perhaps through example and advice, riding this particular wave.
- Feature ideas are everywhere you look, once you know how to look for them. If your client is in the paperclips business, what about a survey to find out the 10 most unusual ways a paper clip has been used?

Feature construction

There are four basic steps to get a feature idea off the drawing board to completion.

Step One: Getting started

- Know the audience/media you want to target.
- Brainstorm ideas, try to link with subjects you know will interest the reader or turn today's news into tomorrow's feature; start with a given day's news and try to turn the specific news event into a generalised feature idea suitable for tomorrow's papers. Here's an example of how this works:

News story	News feature idea
The Bank of England has raised interest rates for the third time in six months.	How to shop around for fixed rate mortgages to prevent negative equity.
Jamie Oliver's campaign for more healthy food in schools has gathered national momentum.	Is Britain a nation of unhealthy eaters? Use some case studies.
Violent crime figures have shown an increase of 5% in the last 12 months.	Who are the people most at risk from violent crime in society?
Anti-Bullying Week is pushing the message that no child should have to tolerate being bullied and that parents and teachers should be part of the solution.	Telltale signs – how parents can recognise if their child is being bullied.

Step Two – Decide on feature type

What category is your feature going to fit into?

- News feature
- Cover feature
- Personality (or company) in profile
- Case study or application story
- Picture feature
- Research study
- Historical feature
- How To
- 'Soft' feature.

Step Three – Planning your feature

For the process minded, the following general guidelines are worth bearing in mind when thinking through a feature idea:

- Start with thesis or a theme and explore it (your controlling idea). The feature needs to go somewhere other than round in diminishing circles – this is a surefire way to lose a reader's interest. You might say that here you are planning the trajectory of the feature.
- Set the stage. Organise all details from your notes. Examine each and review which will best convey what you want to stress in the story. Once you've set the scene, think of your descriptive eye as a camera that can zoom in for a tight focus, then pan back for a sweeping view of the stage.
- Try a paragraph plan, in which you set out the feature content block by block and then flesh them out with detail that brings each to life, including quotes.
- Pay particular attention to your headline and lead. The headline should be expressive and make an impact, the first paragraph an intriguing mix of fact, colour and questions that pulls the reader into the story.
- Pay attention to style. Form can never replace content, but it is through your attention to and use of style that you will develop your own unique voice. With time your voice will become recognisable.
- Present information, opinions, and quotes that flesh out the thesis and which add force and colour to your argument.
- Bring the piece, and therefore the reader with it, to a conclusion that does not leave it open-ended. No reader wants to have a half digested meal.

Step Four – Feature structure

Before you write, it will help if you work out a running order – and stick to it. This should ideally include your paragraph plan, including your background information sources and people who you are intending to quote or reference.

HEADLINE
A good headline is what gets the feature noticed. Five times as many people read the headline as those that read body copy. Use an attention-grabbing headline with a strong message and try to keep it short.

LEADS and INTROS

Must follow on from the heading but, unlike news releases, you do not have to tell the whole story. There are a variety of lead options open to the experienced feature writer.

Anecdote

Notice specific details: 'In the early evening of November 21, 1985, Rehab Amer, a doting mother living in a largely Muslim suburb of Michigan, had just bathed and dressed two of her three young children, and was putting her two-year-old son Samier in the tub when the phone five feet away began to ring. "Mama will be right back," she told Samier, as she moved through the bathroom door to pick up the receiver. Then she heard a thump.

Feature on wrongful conviction for child death. Tim Reid, *The Times*

Question

Ask and answer: When was the last time you got suckered into something you didn't want to do? Perhaps you ended up working late, again, or agreed to take on an assignment that you really didn't have time for. Or maybe you arrived at a work meeting with a firm idea of what you wanted, only to leave with a completely different point of view in mind. If this applies to you, the chances are you've been in the company of a master persuader.

Feature on the art of convincing others. Rebecca Hoar, *Management Today*

News driven

As the next general election draws closer, it is worth examining the management style of the man who has held the UK's top job for eight years and looks odds-on to retain it for a few more. What sort of system has he put in place for those who will occupy 10 Downing Street after him?

Feature on Tony Blair's management style. Robin Cook, *Management Today*

Contrast

Juxtapose detail: Before this August, when I thought of Colombia, I thought of cocaine. That and the fat figures of Botero, the dreamy hyper-reality of Garcia

Marquez, news stories of guerilla war and paramilitary terror, drug eradication programmes, illegal immigration, and the horrific violence and social atomisation that Doris Salcedo witnesses in her haunting, deeply poetic work. But, Botero and Salcedo aside, it was not a country I associated with art.

Feature on contemporary art in Colombia. Joshua Mack, *Modern Painters*.

Historical

The Timberland story began in 1972 when a maintenance man in a small shoe factory in New Hampshire pleaded for a waterproof boot.

Company profile of Timberland showing how the company is boosting sales by being socially responsible, *Sunday Times*.

Quote lead

Use words: "I have the worst job in the Army." Chaplain Col. William J. 'Bill' Hughes spoke with his trademark, gentle Tennessee accent. But he didn't smile. His new job – in the event of a ground war – will be to minister to Fort Hood families whose loved ones have been killed in action in the Middle East.'★

Pun

Investment bankers have written themselves a blank cheque over bonus payments.

Then and now

Forty years ago Barney Hull was a trainee reporter on a small and little read local newspaper in Newcastle. Now, from his office on the top floor of the prestigious Hull Tower in the heart of the city, he manages a newspaper empire that spans the entire North of England.

The feature body

Good features are a joy to read. They paint a picture in words which draws the reader in and keeps him there. The copy flows, the sequencing is sure footed and the linkage between ideas and arguments is strong. Some examples of linking techniques:

- Start with a short sentence. (This makes it easy for the reader to know where the argument is leading.)
- Mention an idea or phrase at the end of one paragraph…pick it up in the next paragraph
- Introduce people before quoting them

Quotations are a good way to provide colour and bring copy to life. People quoted in feature articles tend to be reported in the present tense ('she says', 'he reveals').

If you pose a question, or set out to explore an argument, ensure you bring it to a logical conclusion.

If you are presenting arguments for and against, don't go back and forth between pros and cons. It is far less confusing to present all the arguments in favour together and all the arguments against together.

Avoid long blocks of text as they are not easy on the eye. (Remember a paragraph which spans the screen of your computer, will probably be constricted into column widths when it appears in print.)

Too many numbers or statistics included within paragraphs of text are difficult to read, so use tables or graphs, or highlight essential numbers in separate boxes or charts.

The summary

The writer needs to exit a feature with a punch, rather than a whimper. Unlike news stories, where information is communicated in a strict order of importance, features have to make a final impact. The ending should provide resolution, tie up loose ends, and leave the reader feeling that the writer knew where they were heading all along. When a conclusion is required, make sure that your reader knows that the article is finished. Don't just trail off lamely. Here are some techniques:

- Look to the future

William Blundell, author of 'The Art and Craft of Feature Writing, New Amercian Library, 1988

One cannot hope but wish, whatever has happened between the two families, that her God, or the Stamper's God, will bring peace and reconciliation to Rehab Amer.

The Times.

• Keep a quotation in reserve

"I'm proud of what we do. But look around. One child in five goes to bed hungry in America every night. It's inexcusable. For all the good we do, look around: good ain't good enough."

Jeff Swartz, CEO of Timberland, Sunday Times

• Refer back to an issue or theme

It's true that, if done well, running the country the way one runs a business can improve efficiency. But the checks and balances of democracy need to be in place if it starts to unravel.

Management Today

• Link back to the opening

Ultimately, it comes down to knowing what you want, understanding what works for the other person and getting the message across clearly without steamrollering the listener. If that hasn't persuaded you, nothing will.

Management Today

How PR features work

PR departments and consultancies generally become engaged with features in the following ways:

Commissions: This is where a features editor on a magazine or newspaper calls up and asks whether your client would like to contribute a piece to a forthcoming issue. Your answer to this is 'Yes', following which you may have a brief discussion with the journalist, to be followed up with a written brief which gives a short synopsis and details of word count and deadlines. Whilst you are likely to write the resulting piece, it is likely to be bylined under your client's name.

Pitching an idea: In this scenario you will probably sit round as a team and brainstorm some feature ideas which might appeal to three or four of your key target press. Your discussion will be informed by your knowledge of the magazine and its readership. What issues are topical? What are the preoccupations of the readers? Where is your client qualified to make a contribution? Based on your conclusions, the team can flesh out their ideas by putting together a synopsis for each feature idea, which can then be pitched over the phone to the editor. Pitching, or selling, feature ideas is an acquired skill which cannot be bluffed.

Forward features lists: These lists, which contain a schedule of features planned by a publication over the year, are usually fertile ground for the PR with a saddlebag full of ideas. Often, the schedule will contain planned articles on products, services or business sectors where your client has something interesting to say and some value to add to the debate. Take advantage of these ready-made opportunities and pitch ideas at the features editor in good time.

Case studies: These take the general to the specific. They can often be sold in independently of a broader idea and slotted into a wider piece being planned by the journalist. Case studies usually benefit from an illustration or photo which helps to sell them. Good slots for case studies in nationals, for example, would include dedicated personal finance or health sections, which are always looking for real-life examples.

Style and Impact

As I have already suggested, your feature cannot be a triumph of form over content. However, style is critical. The difference between copy that is leaden and prosaic and copy which leaps from the page – imaginative, upbeat and pithy – is everything. No one wants to read a laundry list when they don't have to, so it is up to you to use style in a way which will excite the reader.

Only you can develop your 'voice'. However, you can learn by reading how others put features together and borrowing the phrases, tricks and constructions that seem to work best for them. Don't be shy! Someone else will do just the same with your copy if you get good enough. And there are some style tips to follow which make good sense – here are just a few of them.

Show and tell. Look at your feature in a visual way, in terms of the images it constructs in a reader's head. This will lead you to show rather than tell all the time, which becomes boring. Instead of saying, for example: 'he was absolutely delighted with the results..' better to show delight, as in: 'smiling broadly, he hugged each one of the team in turn …' This second phrase shows delight.

Avoid describing the physical characteristics of your setting or subject with vague modifiers. Such words as tall or short, fat or thin, for instance, will be interpreted differently by people.

Use the active voice. This, particularly where applied to headlines, has much more power and impact than the passive. Use of the passive voice, whether in news or features, has the effect of slowing a piece of writing down, and thus reducing the impact.

Avoid clichés. These show your knowledge to be shallow. Take a cliché and rework it to cause the reader to do a double take. Instead of "fame and fortune," you may use "fame and misfortune."

Play with words. All good writers enjoy having fun with words – the shape, the sound and the context. If you are having fun, so will your reader. Play with figures of speech. Use similes (verbal comparisons that use like or as), metaphors (verbal comparison, but the relationship is implied rather than stated) or personification (when you attribute human characteristics, feelings or behavior to nonhuman or inanimate objects.)

Vary sentence length. Consider sentence fragments or a single word for emphasis. A shorter word containing the same information as a longer word or a phrase is almost always more powerful. Gather more than you will need in the reporting stage; writing will be easier.

Top Tips To Improve Your Chances!

- Fact selection is everything. A good writer is merciless in deciding who gets into his article. Each person must be instrumental to the theme or the story or be excluded.
- Quotes, too, are better pruned and pared. Favor the short and sharp over the long and dull, and trim the statement down to its intrinsic meaning.
- Readers (and listeners) can't absorb endless numbers or statistics, so be sparing with the ones you choose to highlight. It is better to use one 'silver bullet' number than four or five lesser ones.
- There is tendency to load everything down with adjectives and adverbs when what you really want to do is strip the copy back to the precise sense.

- The story flows better if the writer varies the length of paragraphs and uses a variety of attribution.
- Write in the style of the publication and keep to the number of words requested. Nothing is more annoying for the editor if a piece is way over the agreed word count and then has to be subbed down to fit the available space.
- Don't forget to include illustrations. These can be digital photos, high resolution colour or black & white prints, graphs, charts or even screen grabs from relevant websites.
- Move your story along with descriptions of what happened, quotes from people involved in the issue, and details that place the reader in the midst of the action. Make sure your ending is meaningful. Your closing words should make an impact on your readers and tie the various strands of your story together.
- A powerful quote can often make for a good ending. Or you may want to come full circle and refer back to a word or an image used in your opening sentences.

FEATURE WRITING EXERCISE I

Chocolate — The true food of love

It is one month before Christmas. As a PRO for Chocmaster you are tasked with promoting the company's range of chocolate products to consumers. You approach one of the major supermarket magazines and are commissioned by the features editor to write a 400 word *milestone feature*. Here are some facts and opinions you have already gathered. You might consider a discussion on the merits of different types of chocolate and confectionery; the history of chocolate consumption; analysis/opinions on the confectionery industry in Britain; sales/consumption; obesity/health; dental health.

Business

The British chocolate industry is worth £3.6 billion a year. Chocmaster expects to sell £160 million worth of its Christmas variety packs. The average Briton eats 16 kg of chocolate per annum.

History

The Aztecs of central America used cocoa beans to prepare a hot, frothy drink that had restorative and religious purposes. The emperor Montezuma supposedly drank 50 goblets a day. Impressed by its mythical origins, the 17th century Swedish naturalist Linnaeus gave the cocoa tree the botanical name "Theobroma" – gift from the gods.

Henry Stubbes wrote a book in 1662 called *The Indian Nectar, A Treatise On Chocolate*. In this he railed against those "ignorant chocolatemakers" who adulterate the food's purity with alien ingredients. In 1664, Pepys records going to a London chocolate house. He spells it "jocolatte", which suggests cheery milk.

Part of chocolate's allure can be explained by its stimulant properties. Casanova was reputed to drink it before going to bed. Since the late seventeenth century in Europe, chocolate was consumed as a drink (like coffee). Chocolate in its modern, solid form was only invented in the mid-nineteenth century.

Gastronomy and chemistry

Science suggests that chocolate may be the food of love. What has not yet been explained is why women appear more susceptible than men. Nor whether chocolate is correctly classified as a food – not a drug.

Cocoa butter (the main constituent of chocolate with sugar), melts at a point just below body temperature, so that it liquidises in the mouth. Phenylethylamine is the chemical substance in chocolate that appears to confirm the 'sex substitute' theory of chocolate consumption. It seems to trigger the brain's 'reward pathway'. Some of the other chemicals in chocolate (there are more than 300) act on the brain's specialised cannabis-receptors.

"I've been addicted to chocolate for as long as I can remember," says Gail Simmons, a 37-year-old travel consultant. "It's not a food to me – it's a drug. Milk chocolate with its high sugar content does not count. It has to be chocolate with a high cocoa butter content. When I eat good quality chocolate, I feel a sense of wellbeing flooding through me."

Check your answer against the version in Chapter Thirteen.

CLEAN WASH OR GREEN WASH?

You are writing a feature for a new consumer magazine called *Going Green*. *Going Green Business* is aimed at consumers with an interest in purchasing and using environmentally-friendly products. You have been handed three press releases and told to see what you can come up with. This is a classic *news feature* assignment where you are asked to display your journalistic skills to act as an expert filter and opinion former for the readers.

Three companies are launching environmentally-friendly washing powders in the same week.

- Brand X, from a small 'Green' company claims that it does not use phosphates. Brand X is 25 per cent more expensive than non-green powders.
- Brand Y, from one of the large conglomerates, claims that it uses 30 per cent less chemicals and washes at low temperatures. Brand Y costs 17 per cent more than non-green products.
- Brand Z, an in-house brand of a large supermarket, says it does not use enzymes or optical brighteners, but washes at higher temperatures. Brand Z costs 10 per cent more than non-green powders.

You do some reporting and gather the following information:

- "It is impossible to say from the labelling on these products whether they are environmentally friendly or not," says T H Expert, of Friends of the Earth. "Guidelines on packaging must be strengthened if consumers are to be able to become informed purchasers of environmentally safe products."
- "Our product may appear to be priced higher, but it is actually cheaper than our original product, because you only have to use half as much," says M A Kasale, marketing manager for Brand Y.
- "Our product is safe. I don't know if the other companies can make that claim. They may be an improvement on earlier products, but that's as far as I'd be prepared to go. You can see how serious they are about the environment by the fact that they're still selling their old products," says M R Clean, marketing manager for Brand X.

- "We don't say we're all the way there yet, but it's a start. We can't just withdraw our old products because customers are very attached to them. Besides, we're not saying they're bad, just that this is better. By the way, did you know that the packaging on our products is made 90 per cent from recycled paper?" says I N Store, marketing manager for Brand Z.
- "There's no question about it. The market at which these products are aimed is prepared to pay a premium for so-called safe products. By this time next year every major soap manufacturer will have a green product. Then things will get really interesting because the shops will have to decide which ones to stock. If they push some of the old winners out you'll know the green movement is getting some teeth," says A N Other analyst of Ever So Clever market research.
- "This is a passing fad," says C Y Nic, marketing manager of Supa Soap, which does not have a green soap product. "No one has proved conclusively that domestic detergents contribute significantly to pollution. Mark my words, these products will be gone in 12 months."
- "Too expensive," says one housewife, approached at a London supermarket. "I'll try them, but I can't help wondering if I'm being conned," says another. "How come they're all doing this now?" asks a third.
- "We are still evaluating these products. We will only be able to stock two of them. The demand for this type of product is variable from location to location," says S T O'ckist, buyer at Sainsbury's.

Check your answer against the version in Chapter Thirteen.

Media Interviews and Presentations

Role of the media interview; anatomy of a spokesperson; the interview game plan; the media environment; the rules of engagement; interview architecture; your message & your story; planning for the interview; presentations & speeches; judging the occasion; the middle of a presentation; the end of a presentation.

Role of the media interview

Effective spokespeople, those who can communicate a message with conviction through the media and influence their target audience accordingly are a cornerstone of many public relations and media relations strategies. Almost every media game plan will have a strand aimed at setting up interviews for a number of spokespeople to talk about issues, products, services or alliances and to comment on relevant industry or political decisions. These days, organisations which are on the way somewhere want to capture their *share of voice* or mind and, to do this, need their top people to carve out a public persona as effective ambassadors and communicators and as the human face of sometimes opaque or complex issues. Organisations with stellar media performers at the top have a massive advantage when it comes to putting their story across; just ask the Virgin PR team what Richard Branson delivers for the Virgin brand, or Martin Sorrell for the advertising giant WPP. Both cultivate media personas in a way that is planned and methodical rather than accidental.

It is very few organisations and individuals these days who are actively managing their profile who do not address the media interview as a primary vehicle for connecting with target audiences they need to reach. Any politician, for example, who is launching a major new initiative or who needs to defend a political decision will make it a priority to appear on BBC Radio 4's the *Today Programme* or *Newsnight*, the TV equivalent, because they are both flagship shows with a national audience. Get your message across with conviction in this arena and you have already made a significant impact on shaping attitudes and influencing opinion.

Likewise, a company CEO needing to explain year-end results to financial analysts and institutional shareholders will inevitably try and tell the story behind the numbers to the *Financial Times* in order to get the message across to as many of that audience as possible at once. In doing so, both individuals will be taking risks, upside and downside. The margin between success and failure, triumph and disaster, is always about what happens in the empty space between the journalist and the interviewee. Indeed the risk reward profile of the media interview is probably higher than with any other single link in the PR chain. The role of the PR consultant is to try and maximise the upside and minimise the downside risks associated with those interviews.

Anatomy of a spokesperson

To a certain extent, we can say that great spokespeople and commentators are generally made, rather than born. To that end, these days it is rare that any PR team will send out a spokesman who has not received some media training. Even some basic training in the dos and don'ts of the media interview, how to put across a message and frame answers in a media friendly way will make a massive difference to performance, and therefore achieving the interview objectives.

Role models, both good and bad, abound. We know what convincing spokespeople look and sound like because we see them nightly on our TV screens, hear them through the radio and read their views and responses on the printed page all the time. We think, even subliminally, 'that was effective, I really got the guy's point; he wants action on this issue and I understand why.'

Equally, we have seen the downside – often frozen in perpetuity on YouTube – for so-called experts who are not well briefed, seem not to be in possession of the facts, cannot answer a straight question and do not have an opinion to express on issues that should be of prime concern to them. They can sometimes take a big fall, almost instantaneously affecting their own and their organisation's reputation.

But, as PR consultants, if we know that effective spokespeople are a central part of the media relations strategy and can make or break a media campaign, how do we take that knowledge forward and translate it into action? What intrinsically makes a spokesperson an asset rather than a liability, for example? If we can break the role down into a consistent set of characteristics and attributes, we can actively increase the value of our media assets.

As part of allowing us to actively manage upside and downside risk, media training enables us to operate within a set of parameters that informs just these kinds of judgements. Whilst we can never replace flair or natural talent, we can certainly understand how to move into the realm of the opportunistic and effective.

The interview game plan: confidence, control and credibility

It is unlikely that anyone having to regularly face up to a media grilling will be a natural; nearly all will have been media trained in the techniques required to pull off an interview and get something positive out of it. An effective interview hinges on three attributes: *confidence; control; and credibility:*

- Confidence enables a spokesperson to go into an interview as an equal and enthusiastic participant
- Control means the ability to communicate the agreed message clearly
- Credibility is about the audience being able to find the spokesperson authentic and on top of their subject.

The concept of 'control' includes managing demeanour, presentation, language, message and handling of questions. Most important, it means taking an active role in steering the interview towards the corporate objectives rather than the reporter's – creating and seizing opportunities to assert that agenda, rather than being directed and controlled in a passive sense by the questions that are asked.

For a client to function successfully as a spokesman, the PR consultant has to reassure himself that a set of basics are in place. These basics are in fact prerequisites for the job; imagine them as being CV essentials:

- Understanding and knowledge of the basic organisational numbers: employees, turnover, number of offices.
- Knowledge of the core products and services. Think about the questions: what are your core products? What differentiates them?
- Knowledge of the key markets: Where are you on the map? What is your purpose in being there?
- Knowledge of your job: What do you do? How do you do it?

- Some understanding of the key issues with which the company engages: If you are a car manufacturer, for example, you should expect to cover the green agenda, carbon emissions, fuel poverty, oil prices, road safety, and so on.

Nailing these basics are so important because they drive right to the heart of your credibility. You can prepare a client for interview and cover all the tough questions likely to come up, but you must equally cater for the interviewer who shifts ground to cover a really simple question, for example, an innocent query as to the company's size or best-selling product. How will it come across when the interviewee cannot, for example, remember the size of his company's workforce, or recall an important product launch only three months prior? To that extent, credibility is a fragile commodity – it can vanish quite easily on the turn of a simple question.

Over and above these basics, it is the PR consultant's role to put together a few simple but clear *positioning statements* on key issues that an interviewee would be expected to have an opinion on. For example, if you are a homelessness charity promoting a new awareness campaign, you would be expected to have a position on related issues such as housing policy, healthcare, social services rough sleeping and the benefits system. Being unable to express a view about an issue directly related to your business when asked destroys credibility and diminishes your perceived status.

The media environment

The UK Leveson Enquiry in 2012 brought the role of the UK media more into focus than ever before. Apart from showing up dubious practice in the field of news gathering – phone hacking, for example, was portrayed as endemic – it confirmed that the news media are a pervasive and powerful influence across all levels of society. News media all share one characteristic, a hunger for information, to be first with the story, and the power to make and break reputations.

In recent years, satellite television and the Internet have spawned a truly global 24/7 media environment in which big news is worldwide within seconds. This has increased the challenge for organisations to manage their news agendas and control their messages more effectively, and so protect reputation.

The proliferation of news channels and outlets, with related competitive pressure to be first with the story, has fuelled the growth of sound-bite journalism: the packaging of information in ever-briefer formats. A decade ago, the typical length of a spokesperson's interview sound bite in a TV news story was 15-30 seconds; today, the average is 10-15 seconds (that's around 45 words maximum).

Even in lengthier formats, news information becomes condensed. In most cases, responses will be edited by reporters and then are likely to be cut further by a sub-editor or producer. Then the reader, or listener, may self-edit news consumption by taking in all, or just part, of the story (how many times do you just scan headlines or read just the first paragraph or two?).

Further, intense competition for viewers and readers has led to a blurring of the line between news and entertainment. On the one hand, this has prompted more so called 'soft news' (See: Chapter Six: Working the News Agenda); on the other hand, it has focused more on controversy, sensationalism and investigative journalism.

In fact, the media most often define news as controversy or change, at least as something that has disrupted the normal course of events. In most cases, we will want to avoid or defuse areas of controversy in the media. But unless we can describe some type of change – a new product, service, policy initiative, or shift in direction – or take a controversial position, we may find that an interview doesn't necessarily yield news coverage, or at least coverage that contains your message and desired positioning.

The rules of engagement

Long-term contact with individual journalists is about mutual interest. If the journalist feels that you are reliable and can provide accurate and interesting material about what's going on behind official statements, you will become a significant source of information.

Longer term relationships with journalists will inevitably draw contacts into the minefields of off the record and non-attributable statements. Used correctly, these journalistic conventions can get your version of events into print. The reason these approaches often end in tears is the frequent misunderstanding of what the terms stand for. These rules of engagement are:

On The Record

Any conversation with a journalist is on the record unless agreed otherwise. Whatever you say may be quoted and attributed to you and your organisation.

Non-Attributable

If you wish your comments to be non-attributable, they will be quoted, but without a name or position attached to them. 'Sources close to the company' or 'informed sources' is the usual convention for the non-attributable statement.

Off The Record

An off the record statement is for the journalist's information. It serves to guide further inquiries on the subject. The journalist may cite the content of an off the record statement, but it will appear in print as his opinion.

Everyone seems to have a different take on how to apply these rules, but mine is simple. If you do not want what you say to be reported, *then don't say it*. Take the view that anything you say to a journalist will be on the record. That way, the mind focuses very clearly on what you will or will not talk about.

Interview architecture

Interviews don't always look and feel the same. At a very basic level, television, radio and print formats are very different from each other and present the interviewee with different opportunities and challenges. For example a television interview, unless it is part of a debate within a programme like *Newsnight*, is likely to be no more than around two minutes, whether it is live or recorded. For a live national news programme, it will be much shorter than that, say around 45 seconds. At this length, your interviewee only has time for a sound bite and a key message, so technique becomes paramount if you want to get a message across and answer a question.

Conversely, if you are being interviewed by a print publication, lets say your leading trade magazine, then you can expect up to an hour face to face over the course of a press briefing to cover many subject areas and in great depth, as the journalist will have the time and the knowledge to go much deeper into the topics that interest regular readers.

Part of the preparation process, therefore, and central to the media training idea, is to prepare and practise for different types of interview, so that you vary the interview medium and also the content. This approach helps your clients to become much more fluent in their ability to handle a range of questions, lock in the knowledge areas that they need and polish their answers so that they fit to the right length and contain at least one clear message.

Learning and doing need to be at the heart of any training exercise, so the media training formula sets out to put trainees through a realistic range of interview simulations, using different formats, varied interview lengths and a mix of content to see how effectively a trainee can put across their story in a number of different contexts.

Lets look at an example of this. Say, for instance, that your client is a London-based housing association, whose business is the provision of social housing to those who cannot afford to access the mainstream London property market. The client wants to promote its services to existing and potential customers in South London, at the same time wishing to get across key messages about value for money, efficient use of subsidy, the availability of new stock and so on. Before the media relations campaign kicks in, it would make sense to run the CEO and any other spokespeople through some simulated interview scenarios to test how they perform under realistic conditions. To make these interviews authentic, I would hire a radio and television studio, or at least a camera operator, so that I can provide trainees with playback and related analysis of performance.

The strategy behind these interview scenarios would be to start off testing the credibility of the spokesperson by asking simple questions which require a factual answer. If the spokesman cannot marshal the facts, his or her credibility is called into question very quickly. The time to find this out is before and not during the live interview. As the simulation process continues, so the difficulty of the interview formats is ratcheted up, providing an increasingly tough performance test.

SCENARIO 1: DOWN THE LINE (REMOTE) PHONE INTERVIEW WITH LOCAL PAPER, SIX MINUTES RECORDED.

A reporter from South London Press, Janet Doe, is doing a piece for the online paper and hard copy edition on housing shortages in South London and options for accommodation. As part of the feature, she wants to cover the role of housing associations, and has decided to include a 250 word profile on Yore Housing Association. She doesn't have time to come in to the offices so arranges a down the line, fact-finding interview:

How much housing stock does Yore Housing Association provide in South London?
Who can become a tenant?
How do you get on the list? What is the waiting time?
What services do tenants get?
What proportion of tenants are buying their own houses?
Just how bad is the housing situation in South London?

Think for a moment how you will sound as a spokesperson if you cannot answer these basic questions about who you are and what you do. Your credibility will drain away so quickly that the interview will be cut short. The lesson here is to put together a basic *'cheat sheet'* that sets out some essential numbers and facts you need to know to be credible. It should be kept at the interviewee's elbow; with print and radio, a client can even refer to it and either way will not be caught out on the basics.

In the second interview, which moves from print to radio, the stakes are increased somewhat when the interviewer asks the client to speculate on some issues and topics about which he may have a view, or may not. In any event, he has to ensure that his views are not confused with the housing association's. He has to remember that he is being interviewed in his capacity as a housing association representative; unless he actively steps away from this persona during the interview, his views will by default become official ones. What is the policy, then, on directly answering questions that have an overtly political agenda? This is one example of an issue that needs to be established prior to the interview:

SCENARIO 2: IN-STUDIO RADIO INTERVIEW LIVE (FOUR MINUTES) FACE TO FACE WITH PRESENTER

BBC London Radio 94.9, The 'Drivetime' with Eddie N. show has asked for an interview with Yore Housing Association as part of a debate on housing in London and the overall quality and accessibility of housing services and stock. He wants to know whether the housing association model should be extended further, or whether it is a diversion to take the burden of social housing away from politicians.

Intro: Now I have with me Mr Client Name from Yore Housing Assocation, one of London's biggest providers of housing stock, with over 3,000 homes in three boroughs under management. Some of these homes are rented and some are in the process of being bought by tenants.

What are the main reasons people come to you to access housing?
Do you think Yore Housing Association offers value for money?
Residents' satisfaction with repairs, access to services and customer care are all weak service areas, aren't they?
What are you doing about improving your services?
Is housing a political issue? Should it be?
Is Coalition social housing policy more progressive than Labour's was?

You can see that a swathe of this second interview is asking the interviewee to speculate and give views on subject areas where they may not feel qualified; the interview also makes an assumption – which must be corrected – that your service levels are weak; this may or may not be true but that is not the point. The trick here is to decide, prior to the interview, what subjects you will and will not talk about. Usually speculation and hypotheticals do not hold much promise and are better avoided. Easier to say: "Sorry Eddie, I don't really feel qualified to comment on Coalition housing policy, I prefer to stick to issues where I feel qualified to give a view."

The third interview scenario ramps up the stakes even further, asking for a response – in a live interview – to an accusation that may or may not be true. In this case, it is a reference to the London riots in the summer of 2011. How would the interviewee handle the potential downside risk of this interview, yet still communicate a positive key message about the Association and the work it does?

SCENARIO 3: THREE MINUTES ONE-ON-ONE TV INTERVIEW STUDIO LIVE

BBC London Tonight is doing a piece on action being taken against identified looters in the recent riots. Criminal prosecutions have already passed 2,000 and councils are taking action against those charged and found guilty in council housing. Mike R. has discovered that a number of looters have property under the management of Yore Housing Association.

You manage large tracts of housing in South London, is that correct?

What action are you taking against your tenants who are found guilty of robbing and looting in the recent riots?

What can you tell us about the case of Dave X? This sixteen year old, a convicted looter, lives in Croydon, in one of your houses.

Why have you published nothing and said nothing about your policy on this? Should there be concerted action amongst housing associations? Why isn't there already?

You can see that the tone and content of this interview is almost entirely confrontational and hostile. A great deal could be lost by taking on this interview without very careful preparation. It therefore rests on the PR consultant's shoulders to identify this line of questioning and alert the client to the appropriate risk. There is, in fact, something to play for with this interview, but only for the very experienced who have a wider point to make about housing association policy and who are very confident with the detail at their disposal. Satisfying the interviewer in this case relies on having an approved, official statement which takes on the line of questioning, with the opportunity then to bridge to safer territory when you can get across a more positive key message.

The final interview format in our testing series of simulations is the hardest one of all. Only those spokespeople who are highly experienced and on top of their subject can pull off a convincing live interview that lasts around only a minute. The trick here is to answer the question, but in such a way that it leads on to one key message, in this case about safety.

SCENARIO 4: LIVE 90 SECOND STAND-UP TO CAMERA TV INTERVIEW

Some pieces of concrete cladding have broken off one of the small blocks of flats managed by Yore Housing Association. Unfortunately, one of the pieces of concrete has fallen and struck a woman walking her baby in a pram through a walkway next to the building. The woman has been taken to hospital via ambulance; her condition is reported as critical. London Tonight's Dave D. is with a camera crew on the scene and doing live interviews with witnesses and a piece to camera for the six o'clock news.

Reporter to camera:
Intro: I'm here on the Blue Housing Estate and you can see behind me the flats from which these large blocks of masonry are said to have fallen. Witnesses have told us that the block has required repairs for a long time but that Yore Housing Association has done nothing.

I'm with Mr Client Name from Yore Housing Association.

It seems this was an accident waiting to happen. Do you take responsibility? Neighbours say your record on repairs is not good. Is the state of this block typical?
What's your message for other tenants living in your properties today?
What are you going to do now?

The downside risk of going into any interview is that you are holding your organisation's reputation in the palm of your hand. Just taking the very short interview above, imagine how you, and your organisation, will come across to a TV audience if you do not have responses to reasonable questions in the circumstances. In this last case, the situation is very bad for everyone.

Here, you are in effect already managing a crisis. The right answer of course is to express sympathy for the victims first of all, then make the point that an enquiry is underway to get to the bottom of the reasons for the accident, and finally to communicate a strong message about your safety record. On no account would you admit to anything that was not 100 per cent certain, otherwise you would merely be speculating. After all, if this was happening every week, you wouldn't be in business at all. So the wrong answer would be to allow the interviewer to lead you into the realm of hypothesis and speculation where you have nothing to gain and everything to lose.

Your message and your story

The ability to communicate messages lies at the heart of constructing an effective media interview agenda. Message points are concise thoughts, ideas and arguments that articulate the impression(s) that you most want to leave with your audience. There's no gain in trying to make 20 points in a short interview. Go for just a few as this directs the reporter time and again to the preferred topics.

A good way to begin formulating message points is to determine the specific audience for the interview; remember that reporters and the media are no more than information distribution channels to an audience. The audience might be specialists, at one end of the scale, or the public at the other. The nature of that audience is vital to deciding what story you want to tell, the information to deploy, the language to use and the detail to provide. So define the target audience and what you want them to do, feel or believe.

Do you want them to:
- Support or oppose legislation / action / policy?
- Buy your product or service?
- Support your share price?
- Engage with your organisation in some way?
- Take action on an issue?

Remember that message points must be provable assertions that can be backed up with facts, opinion and explanatory stories. Strategy needs to include anticipating the reporter's questions, from easy to tough, as well as knowing the issues that might arise during the interview – even if they are not directly linked to the interview topic. Journalists have a right to ask any question they like. You have an equal right to answer what you want.

You can never be over-prepared, which is far better than being caught off-guard, especially when a camera is in your face. Ask yourself: "What are the questions I would hate to be asked?" and then work out how you deal with them. Remember the adage: "If you dread it, you could get it."

Lets apply this method to Interview Scenario 4 above. At Yore Housing Association, if you spent some time thinking it through, what would your key message on safety look like? Perhaps something like this:

KEY MESSAGE	PROOFS	STORY
'Our safety record is excellent and we comply with all safety legislation'	1. Government inspectors have passed all our premises safe and issued the relevant certificates. 2. Two of our estates have won awards for quality in the last seven years. 3. We employ a full-time maintenance staff of 50 across all our estates.	In the last 10 years we have only had two minor safety related incidents and both of these were due to unforeseen defects in the construction materials themselves, not in our building standards or use of the materials.

The point about this construction is that your key message, when tested, can be supported by three separate proof points which between them leave no room for equivocation. There can be no doubt that you take safety very seriously. Furthermore, you can supply some detail which shows you take a close interest in the subject, recalling some defective concrete which passed the relevant quality control processes at the time it was used.

Lets take the same formula, and transplant it into the context of value for money, a message which we want to communicate strongly during our second interview scenario, where the question is posed directly and we have to show our value proposition. We might end up with a message matrix like this:

KEY MESSAGE	PROOFS	STORY
'Our service offers real value for money and choice in London's tough housing market.'	1. Our housing stock is excellent quality, constructed to the highest independent standards. 2. We offer tenants a variety of rental and purchase options, giving as much flexibility in ownership and finance as possible. 3. Independent auditors have assessed our provision of services as being in the top quartile in the sector.	Last year our application process was oversubscribed by three times. That means we have a very high level of interest but can't keep up with demand. A lot of these applications come to us via recommendation and word of mouth, like for example the Smith family.'

Through this process, it is possible to develop a set of key messages which together cover an organisation's products, services, culture and people. Whilst not a rigid construction, these message sets form the basis of a media agenda and often bleed further into the communications agenda itself. The ability to communicate them effectively answers the questions: 'why am I bothering to do this media interview?' and 'what do I stand to get out of it?'

Planning for the interview

Preparation is everything

A successful interview is 95% preparation and 5% improvisation on the day. Never agree to an interview without doing some planning and preparation. If you know you can't prepare, decline and pass the opportunity to someone else.

Information

Understand what the interview topic is about, is it news or a feature, why have you been asked, who else is involved, and how it will happen? If it is broadcast, will it be live or pre-recorded, at your site or in studio? Is anyone else being interviewed at the same time? When will it be broadcast? What is the deadline?

Objectives

Always set objectives for the interview. If you don't know exactly why you are doing the interview, don't do it. If you know *what* you want to achieve, you are half-way to knowing *how* to achieve the goal. Define the end audience and exactly what you want to say. Decide on the fundamental point you *MUST* get across in the interview.

Boundaries

Be very clear about what you are prepared to talk about – and what you aren't. These are your no-go zones; they might be about staff, ongoing negotiations, contract details, finances, future plans, and other issues. Prepare yourself to be asked about them – and to close them down instantly, politely and repeatedly. Make sure you're up to speed on issues and potential questions.

Key message points

Your key message or message point(s) are your main focus for the interview. Begin and end the interview with them, and weave them throughout constantly. Say them again and again, in different ways, because repetition helps emphasise them. When you are talking about a key message, use your voice and body language to underline and stress it as important.

Structuring answers

In an interview, you are not having a social conversation that tends to meander its way towards a conclusion. Instead, you are having a structured conversation with a point, inverting the usual social form so that you begin with your conclusion and then explain why and how you arrived at that conclusion. This structure echoes the classic structure of a news story and is just how your answer should be constructed as it helps the journalist put words into a story shape immediately, and gives him the most important information up front.

Using the right language

Keep it simple and say it clearly. You need to talk in terms of reality, and make your thoughts, concepts and opinions come to life. You want to avoid talking in the abstract, in the intangible, and make it real.

Tell stories

You could speak hundreds of words in an extended interview – yet the print reporter might only have space for 300. So of those hundreds you've spoken, which are the ones you'd really like him to use? You can signpost what is important, in words used, voice tone and body language – and in the word pictures you paint or the anecdotes you use.

Balance, control and questions

Journalists have the right to ask any questions they like – and may ask certain questions, or ask questions in a particular style – in an attempt to impose their control over the interview. Part of your mission is to either be more in control and more balanced than the journalist, or to have a 50-50 balance of control. It is not the journalist's job to set the limits of the interview. It's yours.

Giving a good interview can be described as having a conversation with a point. An interview may feel like a conversation and look like a conversation – but it's actually a performance. You are on stage, indulging in some acting to engage and convince an audience.

The most common mistake committed in interviews is to become so fixated by the questions that you lose sight of your own agenda points and become a passive respondent. Don't feel obliged to answer every question specifically. The most effective spokespeople listen to the bigger issue behind each question and address that issue as they choose. This is done through a technique called 'blocking and bridging.'

'Blocking' means deftly avoiding any unwelcome or unproductive question. It may be a hostile or controversial question, an undesirable hypothetical situation or choice, a request for information that you can't disclose or simply something that doesn't pertain to your agenda during a brief interview.

If you're asked a question that is good for you, give it a big answer. If you're asked a tough or unproductive question, you need to deal with it somehow. 'Bridging' means taking the discussion from unfriendly to friendly territory by making a smooth transition from an undesirable question or topic to an area that fits your agenda. Blocking and bridging are accomplished by using smooth connecting phrases such as:

"That's a very good question – but the real issue is.."

"It's not a matter of.."

"Let me start by clarifying.."

"You know, the real question is.."

"That has been an issue, but what's more important is.."

"Let's look at this another way.."

PRESENTATIONS AND SPEECHES

"I have a dream that one day, on the red hills of Georgia, the sons of former slaves and the sons of former slave owners will be able to sit down together at the table of brotherhood,"

Martin Luther King, 28th August 1963, Washington DC

When Martin Luther King stepped up to speak in Washington DC, the civil rights leader and champion of freedom for black people in America must have felt the hand of history upon his shoulder. He might have launched into a long and technical treatise on civil rights and the legislative process to establish true equality in 60s America; he might have dwelt on personalities whom he saw as instrumental in holding up the advances for which he and others had campaigned, and gone on to unleash a negative, embittered diatribe. But instead he made a visionary speech using simple language, driven by a strong and compelling moral case and fuelled by simple rhetoric and mannerisms loaned from the pulpit – repetition, direct appeal, the painting of a series of pictures with words so that people could connect with his vision. The power of this oratory, and its ultimate success, lay in its simplicity, its balance between content and delivery and its consummate understanding of his audience.

Martin Luther King may have made a famous speech on that day; however, history has laid out enough examples of great oratory, Churchill and Nelson Mandela among them, that we can be in no doubt about what is required to make us as an audience sit up and take notice. Of course, great orators are few and far between and most of us will not exactly feel the hand of history on our shoulders in the same way. We will not be declaiming from a platform to an international or even national audience. Much more likely that we will have to plan and deliver something altogether closer to home – a presentation in order to win new business or draft a speech for a client for a business or specialist audience. However, some of the same rules that govern the art of oratory and rhetoric ought to be instrumental in shaping our approach.

Judging the occasion

It is extraordinary in its own way how there could be such a disconnection between what we know works for us and inspires us as an audience and the horrors that we ourselves are prepared to inflict on our own audiences. In the PR consultancy business we are directly concerned with putting together and delivering presentations and speeches, both for ourselves and on behalf of clients. They look to us, as professional communicators, to construct a compelling presentation that captures the audience interest and achieves the chosen purpose. Why do we find it so hard?

There are many books that have been written about successful presentations and I do not propose to offer a re-tread of them all here. However, whatever methodology you import into the process of putting together a successful presentation, it is perfectly clear that if you avoid certain classic pitfalls you are already on your way to at very least a respectable performance.

Rather as with a media interview, it pays to do some thinking about a presentation or speech before you physically sit down to write it. Again, the audience is everything. It dictates the content, the style, the language and the delivery. So the first question to ask yourself is why you are doing the presentation. What is the occasion? Is it going to call for inspiration and improvisation, or is it more process driven and a question of covering the technical bases?

Is it a 'call to action' presentation or speech where you want the audience to go out and do something as a direct result or is it an invitation to simply reflect on a development about which they may be unaware and where you can help them?

And is it the kind of presentation or speech that you want to reinforce with some graphic content, such as Powerpoint slides, or would you prefer to have the audience's attention focused on you, the speaker and what you are saying? Powerpoint, as we know, is probably the biggest single enemy of presentations and speeches; it can stifle, bore, baffle, overcook and bury an audience with detail; it even has its own crushing context in the corporate lexicon, the notorious 'death by Powerpoint'. At the same time, a few finely judged Powerpoint slides in the right places can be extremely helpful to show the detail of a case you are making, perhaps an organisational chart or workflow document which provides clarity.

The first major point to make about presentations, or speeches for that matter, is that they each comprise two component parts, *content and delivery*. Just having one of these components nailed is not enough, you must have both. That means focusing down on what you want to say and how you plan to say it, with neither being done at the expense of the other.

Planning and preparation

"To those waiting with bated breath for that favourite media catchphrase, the 'U-turn', I have only one thing to say. "You turn if you want to. The lady's not for turning."

Margaret Thatcher, Brighton, 10th October 1980.

On balance, doing a great presentation and winging it are incompatible. Conventional wisdom suggests you should allocate one hour to prepare and rehearse for each minute of your presentation. This is how much time it will take to do a good job, in research, planning and most importantly in delivery. It almost inevitably will not be possible to commit this level of attention to a presentation, but the point about preparation is one that stands. There is no-one to blame for poor performance and delivery but yourself.

As a rule of thumb, the attention span of an audience is around 20 minutes. If you plan a presentation or speech which is longer than that, you do so in the knowledge that you are pushing your audience beyond their natural limit. So why do it? If you have a 40 minute slot for a business speech, surely it is a better approach to make a 20 minute speech and then open up the floor to questions, making the second part of the session interactive and engaging? Once the formal bit of the presentation is over, you can then show so much more by engaging directly.

Many business presentations are very dull. If your subject is intrinsically quite boring, why make it more so by using endless bullet pointed copy slides which you repeat as you make your way down the page? This is a total turn-off, and one which we have all sat through in our time. If you choose to use bullet pointed copy slides, the first rule is to differentiate your script so that it doesn't repeat what the audience can already see. When you write your presentation, do it like a video script and put the image on the left-hand side of a column, and the words on the right-hand side opposite. That way, you will cut out repetition and the audience will be challenged rather than bored.

It is worth remembering that if you have access to a screen, you should think about using pictures where you can. If you use pictures, still or video, research suggests that you can double the chances of getting a good hearing. And that is a major competitive advantage. These days, even a decent laptop PC with outboard speakers can give you a proper soundtrack; and video clips or access to a decent wi-fi system will enable moving film or a series of stills.

Either way, rehearsing is an absolute must. The smart move when planning a rehearsal is to do it with one of your peers who can act as audience and critic. Fine tune what you have done to make content and delivery more effective, increase the impact and check the timing.

Starting your presentation

"I stand before you today, the representative of a family in grief, in a country in mourning, before a world in shock,"
　　　　　　　　　　　Earl Spencer, Westminster Abbey, 6th September 1997.

This is the most important part of the presentation and serves two main purposes: to act as an attention grabber for the audience and to let the elevated levels of adrenaline racing through your blood stream settle down, so that you can relax into your presentation. This may well happen while the audience are finding their seats and wondering what is going to happen next. There is no right and wrong attention grabber, but here are some of the standard ones:

- A personal anecdote or story that makes a wider point
- A video clip, but if you use one, make sure that it is less than 60 seconds
- Unusual statistics about your industry or about your audience (the silver bullet!)
- A cartoon.

The middle of a presentation

"Comrades! The cult of the individual brought about rude violation of party democracy, sterile administration, deviations of all sorts, cover-ups of shortcomings and varnishings of reality. Our nation bore forth many flatterers and specialists in false optimism and deceit,"

Nikita Khruschev, 25th February, 1956

A reliable presentation technique is the *rule of three*. The rule of three is based on the technique that people tend to remember three things. In oratory it comes up all the time, for example:

"Friends, Romans, countrymen"

"The good, the bad and the ugly"

"Blood, sweat and tears"

And Tony Blair's call for three priorities: "Education, education and education."

As a rhetorical device, the list of three works more often than not. Think like this: if there are only three points that I would like to leave my audience with, what would they be? There you have the middle of the presentation. All you now have to do is to think of ways of illustrating these points and then you have the bulk of the structure of the presentation.

The end of the presentation

"I have cherished the ideal of a democratic and free society in which all persons live together in harmony and with equal opportunities. It is an ideal which I hope to live for and achieve. But, if needs be, it is an ideal for which I am prepared to die,"

Nelson Mandela, 20th April, 1964

The end is as important as the beginning; it is what your audience will remember. There are a number of techniques that can work well, but they should be all related to the main structure of the presentation. Ideas include;

- An amusing story (one that encapsulates at least one of the main themes of the presentation),
- A high energy video clip,
- A call to action: 'Go out and do something…'

If you are really struggling for ideas, and want to play it safe, you could simply revisit the three main points that you have put forward in the middle section.

Body language

Most presenters, even experienced ones, suffer to some degree from performance nerves. Like an actor about to hit the stage, even when you have given hundreds of performances, the fear never entirely goes away. Perversely, these signs of nerves are actually good for you; they mean you are taking the occasion seriously and your adrenalin is starting to pump. Learn how to harness the feeling, just like actors do. Use your breathing to control your diaphragm and any nervous shakes.

Maintain good eye contact with the audience. Don't keep contact with only one group of the audience. Spread your attention around the room. An idea that works well is 'quartering': divide the room into four parts, pick an individual in each part and look directly at them. And don't ignore the people at the back – make sure you eyeball them as well.

When you get to the lectern, unlock your knees and act as if you were about to catch a ball. It will relax you and make it all flow much more smoothly. You can also anchor one foot against something solid so you don't waver around like a flagpole in the wind.

Keep an open posture, don't slouch, fold your arms or weave about evasively. Audiences can sense uncertainty, so some shyness and nerves are OK. However, a speaker who is physically shrinking away from an audience, or is unwilling to engage wholeheartedly, becomes unconvincing and frustrating.

Remember that an open posture will help your voice tone, modulation and volume, all vital tools to presenting memorably. With confidence you can walk out from behind the lectern and into the audience. Your aim? To dominate the space and make it your own.

Some tips on speeches

Write down your speech, but try not to read from it. If you have written it down and you dry up, you will be able to pick it back up again. When you practice your presentation, do it with a *tape or video recorder* and then play it back to find out which bits sound weak. Then fix them.

Do not read from your notes, unless you have frozen or not prepared. It will sound flat and stilted. If you have learnt your speech it will sound natural and you will even have the chance to ad lib, if the opportunity arises.

Focus on delivery

When you speak, try to speak with passion and enthusiasm and not too quickly. If you speak passionately it will make up for many other shortcomings. The power of pausing in a presentation can be very profound. It will also give you a chance to catch your breath.

Alcohol etiquette

A hangover will be the kiss of death to your presentation. Alcohol can drain all of the enthusiasm from your voice or in turn make you boisterous and seem unhinged. The time to have a drink is *after* a successful presentation.

Check the room

If possible, try and spend some time in the presentation room beforehand. Get to know the room and its acoustics so that you feel comfortable and at home.

Always leave a calling card

You have gone to a lot of effort to produce your presentation. Leaving handouts will reinforce your messages, and will help them to remember your presentation when they look at them again. Always include your contact details so that the audience can contact you.

You can also bring in scanned images of press cuttings, for example, or photographs, which illustrate projects or problems, you are referring to. The memorable presentations are often the ones which combine media successfully, where the speaker knows the subject and the script so well that the delivery seems powerful and natural at the same time. If you are going to move between media, make it seem as seamless and natural as possible – technical hitches are OK for a few seconds but then audiences tend to turn off.

CHAPTER NINE

The PR Launch

Managing expectations; 10-point planner; planning the launch; universal launch elements; shaping the launch proposal; the three-phase model; channel integration; choreographing the launch event; examples & exercises.

Everyone knows a great PR launch when they see one. It makes a major impact and dominates the news agenda and the subsequent media conversation. Just think about the anticipation, build-up and delivery of the latest Apple iPad or iPhone. These consumer products, worshipped as much for their design as functionality, create the kind of waves and consequent queues around the block that clients (and PRs) dream of.

In the same breath, everyone who has witnessed a disaster of a PR launch has had the same thought: 'Thank God that wasn't my client. Where would I be hiding now, with my mobile switched off and an ice pack pressed against my forehead?'

The fact is that the word 'launch' has the capacity to inflict – in equal measure – a mix of fear and excitement into the professional PR consultant. The stakes are immediately raised, in direct proportion to the impact of success or failure. Think of the opening night of a West End play. Think of the reviews. Think 'Box Office!' This is showbiz we are talking about – albeit a more corporate branch.

Launches can make or break products. An unsuccessful launch is not the same thing as writing a poorly received news release or setting up a feature opportunity which appears in print with an ambiguous headline. There is really no such thing as a successful relaunch, and PRs are not generally in the business of being given a second chance by clients to get a launch right. It either works first time or the agency may be heading for the exit – brutal but a fact of consultancy life.

That means – as PRs – we enter the high risk zone. Here, hedging is not an option because the argument is not really about marginal outcomes. No amount of prevarication or justification can reinvent an empty room or zero column inches.

Managing expectations

Clients – being the kind of breed they are – tend to reckon they are sitting on the most exciting product since the telephone was invented. Revolutionary, exciting, relevant, life-enhancing, great value – the list goes on. More occasionally, they understand that there may be limitations to their new product or service. As PR consultants, it is our job to provide them with the best advice we can. We have to begin the launch exercise by analysing the brief they are giving and offering them considered feedback. After all, our heads are on the block as well as theirs. This is the starting gun for managing their expectations.

The following steps are helpful guidelines.

- Talk in depth across the table to the people who have developed the product. What are the features and benefits. What are the USPs? What makes it new, improved, exciting? Does it really have 'sizzle'? Does it pass the 'so what' test?
- Talk also to the sales team that are going to be responsible for rolling it out. What do they feel about it – who are they talking to and what market testing has been done? Is there any research to use to backup the product story and support the launch? How are pre-sales progressing?
- Talk to the marketing team about their thoughts and plans on launch. What go-to-market strategy will they be taking? How does the launch fit with the content and timing of other plans. The most effective launches are *integrated* with other marketing elements.
- What sort of audience demographic is the product or service for? Is it consumer, business-to-business, niche market? Are they A/Bs or D/Es? Is there audience research that we can use which shows the kind of response which might add some science to our launch strategy? If there is, grab it! If not, why not?
- Get a feel for what the client expects to achieve by the launch. Do they anticipate massive sales and prospects pouring through the door or jamming

the phones? Or just the front pages of the nationals or regionals, with massive exposure on regional and local radio and TV as well? Begin shaping judgements early about what is *realistic* and *achievable*.

- Talk to the client about budget and timeline. What is the planned spend and when is the launch date? Is it worthwhile hiring Pink Floyd to do a concert at the Pyramids at Giza, with sponsorship from Pepsi, if the budget is £5,000? Nail down the numbers – this is vital, otherwise you are wasting their time and your own.
- Once you have asked a lot of questions, take the answers and the brief away and start considering the options.

10-point planner

This ten point plan might be helpful to provide a handy reference when the subject of launches comes up. It provides the basis on which to interrogate any proposed launch programme:

- Can I see a 'sizzle' quotient in this product or service? Is it a hard, soft or no launch item? Am I excited by it – does it pass the 'so what' test?
- Can I see at least three ways that I could launch this product – depending on what money was available? If not, why not?
- Is there a celebrity or personality I can imagine who would want to endorse this? And why?
- Can I write a news release about this new gizmo in my head? Can I see the story already?
- Is there something visual about this? Is it funny, poignant, dull or really exciting? Could I create a compelling angle?
- Would a national newspaper journalist cover it, or is it more geared to trade and local papers?
- Is a there a precedent for this type of product launch? Can I find out from agency sources what kind of launch model has been used before? If 'Yes', what lessons were learned?
- Does this client seem to have unrealistic expectations? Perhaps we should sit down and have a frank chat about what I think is possible.
- Is the client prepared to fund the type of launch the product or service needs? Could we work with this client?
- Do we have the capacity to service the level of work required?

Planning the launch

When you sit down with the team to plan a launch, you may feel you are looking at a blank sheet of paper, and in a sense that is true. Your thinking should not be confined. However, in another sense there are some established formats within which you can wrap your ideas and begin to shape them into a programme. The following guidelines are helpful to planning any launch.

The brainstorm

Great ideas are not the sole province of seniors who have been around a long time. They don't have a monopoly on thinking, simply on the company credit cards. So get everyone in the consumer team or B2B team – whichever is relevant – and get round a table. Appoint a facilitator and get a wealth of ideas down on paper. However crazy they may seem, they have value. They enable you to escape confined thinking and be really creative; make sure you use a brainstorming technique that is inclusive.

The consumer launch

A product or service aimed at consumers needs to have clear touching points that the public will empathise with and feel is part of their world. Is there a place or a person who would give the product an identity, endorse its value and relevance and be appropriate to the basic brand values? For example the first annual DOH Flu campaign, designed to get pensioners to sign up for a flu jab, used boxer Henry Cooper to front the advertising campaign. The target group could identify with the man. Is there a clever idea that knits different aspects of the product together and makes it memorable in different ways? Use lateral thinking to explore these possibilities.

The trade launch

Usually this can be a more measured affair, regulated perhaps by a greater emphasis on content than form. We might look for an existing event which lends itself to the launch because of the audience that is already guaranteed. For example, IT manufacturers will use the massive CEBIT exhibition in Germany to showcase new hardware and software developments; motor manufacturers will use the Motor Show in Birmingham to launch new models and accessories.

Be creative about how you leverage existing trade opportunities to your own advantage.

The soft launch

You do not always have to 'go large' when bringing a new product or service to market. It is an option simply to put the word out through your existing distribution networks – via literature, dealers, press releases, a hot line and so on – which lets customers know that they have another choice to look at. Particularly where the 'sizzle' factor is marginal – number 153 in a line of 152 widgets for bathroom taps – you may simply be wasting time, effort and budget organising a massive launch event.

No launch!

This speaks for itself. If you just can't see the value or impact of launching something formally, then say so. It will save many tears later in the process.

Universal launch elements

Most PR launches have universal elements. Why? Because others have proved they work, to a greater or lesser degree depending on the skill behind the planning and execution. In other words, the good news is that there is a formula you can employ. These elements are the basic building blocks of the launch strategy.

The focus

To qualify as a launch, there must be a focus. This means an event; something out of the ordinary must happen to create noise and sizzle. Even if you get the local Mayor and MP to release a hundred balloons from the roof of the town hall, you have a focus, a launch event.

Third-party endorsement

The most successful launches tend to find a personality who will be associated with the product. Why? They provide visibility, credibility and high recall. They add sizzle and make for memorability – a task which is getting tougher and tougher. List five celebrities you can associate with a product launch, for example Alicia Keys and Blackberry. In doing so, be aware that celebrities who have no natural empathy or ownership of the product tend to lack credibility; the reverse is also true.

A photo-opportunity

Again, the best launches tend to embed an element which has a visual pull – either for television or newspaper photographers. Something fun, unusual, exciting or just plain off the wall. There needs to be something to look at. Remember the 118 118 runners underneath the Wimbledon scoreboard?

Media involvement

It is a fine judgement these days whether to organise a press conference, a series of one-to-one press briefings or down the line interviews. However, with both consumer and trade launches the press are a vital component for success. Most clients will still measure success by column inches, film footage and new business enquiries. This is one of the most challenging aspects of the launch strategy and one which needs to be managed very closely.

Information and collateral

You will need to produce information that is accessible in every format, digital and hard copy. This will usually include: news releases; photography; press pack; q&a; spokespeople briefings; and product sheets. Well researched media distribution lists will carry this information to the right people.

Action plan

A highly evolved, blow-by-blow action plan with timed activities, contact details of the major players and someone to manage the itinerary. And what is your fallback position if something goes wrong? Have you considered your doomsday scenario strategy? If not, do it!

The launch team

Get the right mix of people in the agency to do the job, for example:

- an events specialist;
- a media relations whizz;
- a great organiser and co-ordinator;
- a manager/motivator.

Get the team to REHEARSE, REHEARSE, REHEARSE!

Shaping the launch proposal

Agencies involved in launch projects need to be clear – both for themselves and for clients – precisely what the rules of engagement are. When the debrief happens after the event, it will be too late to sit down and say: "But that wasn't what you said you wanted." These general rules must be applied to the launch proposal before activity gets underway.

Objectives

There must be clear and precise objectives applied to the launch (see SMART in Chapter Four: Writing Winning PR Proposals). Everyone, client side and in the agency, must understand and buy into these. Without them, the strategy, tactics and execution will have no context and fall apart. So spell out what the launch needs to achieve.

Success criteria

Agency and client need to agree – beforehand – what constitutes success for the launch programme. How will this be measured? Column inches, radio coverage, sales leads, telephone calls to a hotline or higher measured recall amongst shoppers on the high street? ROI – Return on Investment – is a fact of life these days. Get used to it and build it into the plan!

Launch strategy

This spells out the approach and is, in effect, the plan that both client and agency are signing up to. Any deviation from the plan needs to be recognised as such and noted formally.

The programme

The programme tells agency and client what is going to happen, when, and who is going to do it and take responsibility for it. A detailed programme is important because this is what the client is paying for and it is also what the agency is delivering for an agreed fee. Deliver more for the same fee, result – great launch, financial disaster!

Integration

The PR launch activity needs to be integrated with other sales and marketing activity – for example direct mail, advertising and special promotions. This activity should be accommodated in the timeline.

The timeline

This puts the launch programme into time perspective. It should have a high level of detail, be set out on a spreadsheet and made available to agency and client teams. Update regularly so that activities are ticked off.

The budget

Launches cost money – agency time, bought in costs of items like celebrity fees, venue hires, special promotions and so on. A budget needs to be worked out and agreed at the outset and revisited as the project progresses through the timeline.

The three-phase model

When constructing your launch plan, it can be helpful to look at it in three distinct phases. This focuses the strategic approach and helps breakdown the tactical implementation into more manageable chunks. A model that lends itself to this phased approach might look like this:

Pre-launch

–   Integrate PR activity with other marketing plans, for example advertising and direct mail, to optimise impact and ensure there is no duplication.

- Put together detailed press information, including: news release(s); backgrounder; fact sheets; media distribution lists.
- Media train selected spokespeople if they are not already up to the job.
- Do some selected pre-briefings with primary target media.
- Think about pre-launch 'teaser' campaign which heightens expectations.

'Go-live'

- Watch and listen to the news agenda for the day to check on breaking stories. Could you be aced by something else that might cause you to make a late change in plan?
- Detail breakdown of what action plan is for the day.
- Organise photo-opportunity for mid-morning – the optimum time for dailies.
- Make sure overnight electronic news distribution has happened.
- Set aside somewhere quiet for radio interviews and 1-2-1s.
- Make sure event 'press office' keeps log of enquiries to monitor f/ups and journalist requests.

Post-launch

- Organise f/up stories, photography and down-the-line interviews.
- Capture response details and start to monitor coverage.
- Keep a moving log of reportage & comment to measure tone and acceptance.
- Stay in touch with the client every day to keep them in the loop.

Channel integration

Part of the challenge of maximising any launch impact is to integrate and co-ordinate the use of the various marketing channels that might be deployed as part of the overall sales & marketing strategy. In this context, PR & media relations is just one – albeit powerful – tool in the promotional armoury.

With a consumer launch, for example, it makes sense to roll out an advertising campaign, perhaps backed by direct mail, within a schedule that generates the maximum opportunities to see (OTS) when editorial coverage is also at its strongest. The impact on consumers of getting the same message through two different media at the same time acts as powerful reinforcement to a launch campaign.

On the same principle, the launch might be further reinforced by the concurrent use of direct mail and e-mail to one or more carefully targeted consumer groups. Using a third channel to reach the target audience is a clever way of 'narrowcasting' to maximise the launch reach. What are the other channels which could be deployed in a product launch alongside PR and media relations?

- ADVERTISING: Trade and consumer, success measured through Opportunities To See (OTS), awareness ratings
- DIRECT MAIL: employed to reach named consumers, success evaluated by response rates
- TELESALES: Targeted selling by phone, usually outsourced to experts and judged by direct product sales
- EXHIBITIONS: Trade and consumer shows, where success is measured by footfall, sales leads & enquiries
- PRODUCT DEMONSTRATIONS: Organised in-house to target existing customers and prospects, measured by attendance rates
- ROADSHOWS: Mobile product demonstrations, usually constructed on major city basis, measured by attendance rates and enquiries
- SPECIAL PROMOTIONS: Price offers built into launch sale strategy, judged directly by sales figures

Choreographing the launch event

There is no law that says you have to use an event to launch a new product. However, an event of some kind or other generally forms part of a product launch strategy, particularly where you are demonstrating product benefits that are highly visible. You may choose to identify a particular trade show, or set up a road show or series of product demonstrations either at your own premises or at client sites to complement your overall launch activity.

A relatively small and manageable event at your own premises is often a good way to provide focus for a product launch. You can build other marketing activity, such as advertising and telemarketing, around the event to add further dimensions to it. A step-by-step approach to your launch event strategy should look something like this:

Planning ahead

Plan at least four weeks ahead when you set a time and date for the launch event. Typically, your launch or demonstration might take place in the early evening after work at your offices, if they are reasonably central and convenient. Remember that people who have busy diaries need some notice and you and your team need sufficient lead time.

Send out a signed invitation letter to named individuals. The letter should have a powerful sales message embedded in it focusing on the business benefits of the product but might also highlight the opportunity to listen to an interesting speaker who will be fronting up the event. Follow up the letter with a phone call if you have not heard back within 10 days or so to ascertain interest in attending. Build your list of attendees and non-attendees as you go, and keep it updated. The day before the event, do a final ring-round to check that people are coming.

Getting the right audience to your event is critical. You should do some research amongst your key audiences to see what sort of event would interest them and which they would make time for.

Develop a local database from which to work, comprising existing customers, prospects, commercial partners, perhaps one or two local journalists and any other influencers and specifiers who can contribute to your business. Make sure the database is clean and functional – it is a prime selling tool.

To act as an incentive for the launch, you might want to find a personality to front up the event by delivering a short speech or introduction. This could be a local personality, respected business person or government official. Check with local branches of business organisations, such as Chambers of Commerce and Business Clubs and network with colleagues to look at potential options.

You should prepare a short presentation about the product and the benefits it can deliver, using the product to illustrate them if possible, or inviting guests to have a 'hands-on' session with the product themselves.

Your presentation should be followed by a light buffet, say finger food, accompanied by a glass of wine or a soft drink for people who have to drive home afterwards. The social aspect of the event presents an excellent opportunity for networking and making personal contacts to develop after the event is over.

Provide information for guests to take away with them. *Information packs* should include sales literature, price lists, special offers, discounts and promotions, as well as details for further contact.

You should always follow up your launch event with a letter thanking the guest for attendance and offering further information and to call in or phone when convenient.

Other activity

To supplement your product launch and give it additional profile, you should also develop a marketing package designed to deliver profile for the product and generate enquiries about it. This package can be low-cost, but highly effective. It could include:

- News release with photograph to local and business press.
- A direct mail letter with a response facility to second tier customers or prospects.
- Planning a local or regional advertising campaign in newspapers and relevant trade titles.

LAUNCH CASE STUDY: K+R AND FRIEND INDEED:

Friend Indeed, which came into being in the late 1990s, was the first friendly society to be launched in the UK for many years. It was conceived as a vehicle for offering a unique product – a universal, low cost, 'one premium fits all' insurance scheme for victims of violent crime. Friend Indeed enjoyed the support of some of the UK's largest insurers and victim support groups, and was positioned as a socially responsible measure to create some security of mind to counter the increasing prevalence of violent crime in our society.

Challenge

K+R was taken on to establish an identity for the company and then to launch the product itself, both in very quick succession. We had to establish the credentials of the people behind Friend Indeed, communicate the benefits of the friendly society structure and get across the nature of the product itself, the first of its kind on the UK market. In addition to PR and media relations, K+R was taken on to advise on all other aspects of the marketing, from research to direct mail. Our brief was wide ranging but it was required to be delivered against a limited budget in which immediate value was paramount.

Strategy

The most important objectives were to generate enquiries and to achieve positive media coverage, whilst minimising the opportunity for criticism. K+R firstly focused on making the visual image of Friend Indeed memorable in order to generate strong name and product recall. Because of the sensitivity of the product and the fact that it would be bought through fear of being a victim of crime, we also felt strongly that the product needed a 'face' with whom consumers could identify. This strategy of third party endorsement led us to approach Lisa Potts, the George Medal winning Wolverhampton nursery nurse who had fought off a machete attack on the pupils at her primary school, to front the launch.

Our strategy focused around creating a launch event through which we could make an impact on all target audiences – the major insurers, financial services intermediaries, consumers and social cause groups.

Tactics

A press and photocall event was organised to launch Friend Indeed, featuring Lisa Potts and Sir Louis Blom Cooper, QC, who was on the board of Friend Indeed. Prior to the launch, pre-briefings were held with the personal finance correspondents of all the major broadsheets. Picture desks, radio programmes and TV news outlets were contacted on the day to report on the launch, and a number of interviews with Lisa Potts were successfully concluded. Media relations post-event comprised of regular coverage in women's consumer press and briefings with journalists from national newspaper personal finance pages. A media relations programme was also aimed at trade press to target insurance brokers and personal financial advisers.

An advertising campaign was created using Lisa Potts as a figurehead and implemented across national newspapers and consumer publications. A mobile poster site was booked for the launch event and used for the photocall and then driven throughout London during launch week. After the launch event, the campaign was extended to incorporate regional radio and newspapers. When Lisa Potts launched her book, the advertising campaign was developed to include a special promotion.

Event support was also provided from attendance at the Trade Union Conference to arranging photocalls and interviews at bookstores for Lisa Potts around the launch of her book. Opportunities for third party endorsement were created and Friend Indeed was introduced to the Suzy Lamplugh Trust and Refuge Crisis Line.

Measurement & Evaluation

Around the launch event, 19 interviews took place across national newspapers, radio and television stations, including ITN News, Channel 5 News, BBC Radio 5 Live, Talk Radio, Heart 106.2 FM and the Press Association. Market research conducted post launch revealed 63% awareness of Friend Indeed. The total press coverage reached over 19 million people providing a total advertising value equivalent of four times the fee.

PRODUCT LAUNCH EXERCISE:

Read the PR launch brief below and sketch out some ideas and activities that you think might work and which also would achieve the product launch objectives. Use the ideas and planning models we have looked at in this chapter to give your programme some shape. Remember too that you can add a viral dimension to your launch, together with some highly visual treatments of such an interesting product. Check your answer against the actual case study which you can find in Chapter Thirteen.

MiniPets: the biggest small pets in the world

The Product
Ten collectable, 3.5 cm high, interactive pets that respond to voice activated commands.
The Challenge

Each year, approximately 50,000 new toys are launched, all vying for the media and consumer's attention and aiming to be one of the top toys for Christmas. The PR challenge was to turn the MiniPets range into a collectable craze that would make them one of the best selling toys of the year.

Objectives
- To launch MiniPets as the hottest and most innovative toy product for the year.
- To establish MiniPets as the most talked about toy.
- To assist in creating a kids craze for Christmas.
- To position MiniPets as cool and collectable amongst kids aged 6-10 years.

Execution and implementation

The PR campaign was designed to achieve three different goals:
- **Pre-launch:** to establish word of mouth and playground buzz
- **The launch:** to announce the availability of MiniPets to the UK media/consumers
- **The build:** to maintain a consistently high profile for MiniPets in the run-up to Christmas

CHAPTER TEN

Writing Style

Written communications; the principle of messaging; the role & function of style; using the right voice; appropriate language; principal genres of PR writing; technical process; importance of accuracy; editing & sub-editing; use of grammar; spelling, punctuation; and proofreading.

Amongst other things, public relations is about establishing and maintaining a dialogue with your stakeholders so that you can inform, persuade and influence. The written word is at the heart of this process and it pervades every step of the communications chain, whether through a news release that takes your story to the media or a speech that a CEO makes to an important audience of analysts and investors.

Writing in public relations is not a literary or academic skill but one that is more embedded in journalistic and marketing skills. It is primarily technical and functional and can be taught as a craft. Writing, whether focused on the client or the consumer, is all about packaging up a message and communicating it effectively so that it plays a role in influencing attitudes and perceptions or changing behaviours.

To be an effective and professional PR, you therefore need to understand and deploy the written word and become an effective writer. This is as true in the digital age as it has been in the analogue one, just the medium and some of the tools may be changing.

Written communications

The written word lies at the heart of your *credibility*, whether through the facts or the opinion that you express; there is consequently a high premium on accuracy in PR. The other important thing to realise is that the written word makes what you say a *matter of record*. Going into print is an important step for your organisation or your client in that accuracy is a critical factor in protecting your reputation, whether in making claims that cannot be substantiated or in setting out statements of fact or opinion that open you up to prosecution for *libel or defamation*. There are also strict rules that govern the disclosure and timing of certain types of information, for example relating to companies listed on the Stock Exchange.

Writing in public relations is pervasive and at the heart of every general or specialist branch of the profession, from media relations and consumer PR through to public affairs, investor relations or technical product PR. This chapter is designed to help you recognise and get to grips with the principal ways in which writing is used in PR.

The principle of messaging

Messaging lies at the heart of communications in PR and covers both the spoken and written word. Messaging is the process of defining precisely what it is you have to say to your target audiences and packaging it in such as way that it is memorable and supportable. Sometimes known as 'key messaging', this principle pervades written outputs across the PR disciplines. You might call messages the DNA of your communications.

Messages articulate what you want people to think, feel and say about you and your organisation. They are what you want people to remember and do as a result of your communications (See Chapter Eight, Media interviews & presentations).

Thus it follows that if you are to really understand the written word in PR and its use, you need to familiarise yourself with the principle of messaging being the main driver behind all written outputs. In other words, you are writing for a specific reason and the more its impact can be measured, the more effective your communications will be.

General written communication

In the course of most general PR, written communication can be categorised via the following channels and outputs:

Emails
Letters
Reports
Proposals
Manuals
Magazines
Newsletters
Websites
Marketing materials: (ads, flyers, brochures, e-mailers, posters, websites, banners)

Media written communication

The same is true of written communications with the print and broadcast media:

Emails
Letters
Online newsrooms/press offices
News releases
Features, i.e case studies and profiles
Advertorials
Promotions/giveaways/competitions, etc
Tweets, Blogs

You do not need to become expert in producing all these written outputs, but you do need to be able to recognise them and understand their primary functions.

The role and function of style

Writing in PR, just like writing in journalism, is driven by method. Depending on the nature of the audience you are communicating with, your messages, facts and opinions need to be packaged up in a style and format which is recognisable and thus useful to your target audience. The more effectively you can harness style and form, the better the result your written output will produce, whether a news release targeting journalists and their readers or a research report directed at analysts. Remember though that form cannot replace content.

Many organisations will have a *style guide*. The guide is there to tell you what the agreed approach is to written outputs; they cover everything from word count and format on the page, through to more contentious aspects of grammar and punctuation. Ask to access your own organisation's style guide to get to grips with the details that define your own house style.

In general, style guides are used:

- As a framework to establish a stronger, more consistent connection with the audience
- To get across messages more effectively, foster dialogue and increase interaction
- To make your organisation and its services more accessible and relevant
- To help speak in one voice: to explain, show and tell

However, regardless of individual style, there are certain rules that set guidelines for all outputs used in public relations. It is useful to know what these are so that you get to grips with the different types of writing you will need to recognise and may be asked to reproduce.

Using the right voice

When approaching style, we need to understand the different ways in which audiences can be addressed, as follows:

- First Person – writer expresses his/her views "I have a new product" or "We have a new product" this is most commonly used in emails, newsletters, features, brochures, web pages and is more personal;
- Second Person – writer talks directly to the reader "You will love the new laptop from JD Computing"; this voice is generally used in selling and marketing copy (adverts; promotions; sales flyers and so on)
- Third Person – writer speaks about another person "JD Computing has launched a new laptop." This voice is used most often in news releases, features, brochures, web pages, newsletters – it is less personal.

A good example of understanding how these voices work in practice would be in the writing style used to produce news. Here, you cannot write sales copy as you are not selling anything. News is issued via a third party and is written in the third person to provide objectivity to the content:

NOT "We launched ..."
"JD Computing launched ..."

Don't talk directly to the reader

NOT "You will now benefit from faster web access ..."
"Users will now benefit from faster web access ..."

Sentences should be short and active.

NOT "The laptop was developed by a team of US programmers over a period ..."
"A team of US programmers developed the laptop over a period of ..."

Appropriate language

Using news copy as an example, copy should stylistically be simple, with short paragraphs, short sentences, simple language and ideas which are straightforward rather than highly complex. Paragraphs should contain one message only; copy is more effective when factual and unbiased.

News in particular functions on the concept of third-party endorsement, which underpins all PR. That is to say, an expert opinion expressed about your product or service carries more weight than your own.

Thus NOT "Ford engineers are the absolute best ..."

"Ford engineers have won many accolades from automotive bodies, including the International Association of Automotive Engineers."

- Copy should be plain English and jargon free
- Concepts should be concise and simply explained; sentence structure should reflect the need for accessibility
- It should not require a second reading in order to understand
- The grammar should not be complex
- The copy should be accurate and consistent
- Note: use a spellchecker!

A good tip is to read target publications and deconstruct their editorial style. A rule of thumb in the PR business is: 'if in doubt, write for the intelligent 14-year-old' and you will not go too far wrong.

When you have written copy, you should also ask someone to read for *sense and mistakes* – you cannot reliably proofread your own work.

Principal genres of PR writing

It is helpful to break down the use of the written word into the principal genres used in public relations. With variations and, of course, exceptions these genres could usefully be categorised into the following: *media relations*; *marketing*; *internal communications*; *online or digital communications*; *client communications*; and *technical or specialist*. These genres are characterised by sets of typical written outputs in the following way.

Media relations

These are outputs which are targeted at your end audience by using the media as the intermediary and carrier of the information. The principal written outputs used in media relations would include those we have already examined in this book, still led by the news release and the feature. If you are not reading this book in a strictly linear progression, *revisit Chapter Five: Media Relations*.

Marketing

In this genre of PR writing, we are using the written word to formulate outputs whose direct purpose is to sell. This could be in the form of advertising and promotional copy, sales flyers or leaflets, web copy or even membership benefits or award entries.

More than in any other genre, we are directly addressing the reader, attempting to persuade him or her into making a purchasing decision or commitment. This copy generally employs the rules of selling, packaging up features and benefits around a compelling *sales proposition* and a number of *Unique Selling Points* (USPs).

Copy that sells directly to an audience uses the second person in order to make that direct appeal:

Second Person – writer talks directly to the reader

"You will love the new laptop from John Doe Computing"

In order to be effective, sales and marketing copy needs to be direct and, in addition:

- The proposition and USPs need to be defined
- You need to understand the differences between features and benefits
- Be clear about a call to action: what you are asking readers to do, think or feel?
- Make it easy for dialogue – build in a response mechanism
- Show, don't tell

Internal Communications

Internal communications is an intrinsic part of employee engagement, that vital process which establishes and maintains a dialogue between an organisation's management and its employees. Sometimes, internal communications is the responsibility of the Human Resources department, but it increasingly falls under the responsibility of the PR team.

Internal communication is a specialist branch of PR and uses a variety of tools and outputs. Some of these deploy the written word; they include newsletters, newspapers, magazines, ebulletins, intranets and information leaflets.

Take the Intranet as an example. This is perhaps now the primary tool for employees to talk to each other and through which the dialogue with management is ongoing. Intranets are a process, interactive, evolutionary, and dynamic. Contributing to the content of an Intranet could mean drafting questionnaires and surveys, setting out factual information in step-by-step guides, profiling individuals, running interviews or setting up chat rooms and feedback mechanisms so that employees can engage with each other and with management at the same time. The guiding principles for all internal communications are broadly:

- Publication content should meet the needs of the readership
- It should be relevant, well constructed, accessible
- There should be clarity and jargon free English throughout
- There should be a visual dimension – readers need to look at good design, pictures, graphics alongside words

With the advent of the digital age, PR has moved online along with the rest of the world. In fact, the PR profession is playing a major role in developing online channels and technology into effective communications tools, and developing digital solutions as an intrinsic part of strategic communications.

First generation websites have now been replaced by Web 2.0 and social media, alongside the rise of citizen journalism, user generated content (UGC), blogs and Twitter as a tool for breaking news and forming opinion.

The written word has a major part to play in this evolution. Traditional, hard copy formats may have given way to the digital dimension, but many of the skills inherent in effective communications and PR have remained the same. Most people entering the PR profession are now expected to recognise and, often, manipulate the new digital tools alongside more traditional ones. It is no coincidence that every daily newspaper in the country has an online version, which increasingly acts as the hub for all inward and outward bound information and images.

When you examine news, views and features more closely on the web, you can discern a pattern in what works well. It is this pattern you need to isolate and reproduce, because reading material comfortably on the web requires a different approach to the printed page.

You are aiming for copy that is easy to access, easy to read, modular, active and simple, though not dumbed down. If you want great examples of news and feature writing on the web, go to *the BBC* website (*www.bbc.co.uk*) or the *Financial Times* (*www.ft.com*).

Writing for the web

We want to make sure that our website and essentials are accessible to everyone who uses them. Although design, technology and navigation (how easy it is to find your way around a website) are very important, the style of the content is vital to how easily people can use and understand it.

It is harder to read from a screen than it is from a printed page. People read differently on the web. They scan content, relying on headings and subheadings to guide them. They want quick results and are only a click away from leaving the page, or even the site.

When writing content for websites:

- Make it easy for people to find information, don't make them work too hard
- Make your ideas and sentence constructions simple; complexity is a turn-off
- Make sure you use headings, summaries, captions and links appropriately
- Don't use block capitals, as they can be seen as 'shouting' and are hard to read
- Don't use bold to emphasise words or paragraphs, except for items in the news section

---

Writing online, the focus needs to be on making copy accessible and readily digestible through the use of:
- Headings
- Sub-heads
- Sentence length (15 words)
- Para length (35-50 words)
- Links
- Images

Think about navigation – how will the reader move around the site, from page to page or from story to story? Remember that the attention span in this medium is short. Visitors want instant access and very little complication.

Client communications

In the course of most PRO's jobs, you will be required to flex your writing skills by producing outputs for consumption by your own management or, if you are in a consultancy, by your clients. These will range widely from the recurring and mundane, such as a monthly progress report, to the highly complex and demanding, such as a new business proposal.

The ability to write clearly, concisely and without jargon is the common thread across all these outputs and the main enabler of real two-way communication and dialogue. The same principles that define your outputs in the other genres of PR writing should characterise your output with the client.

The key to this is to realise that, if you are selling yourself as a professional communicator or public relations professional, it is your own reputation which is at risk if you cannot produce accurate and effective copy to put across your ideas, views and recommendations. Thus, accurate and concise copy has an equal job to do internally as well as externally, if it is to be persuasive.

In your organisation, you need to carefully consider the *style guide* that dictates the form and appearance of recurring outputs such as monthly progress reports, meeting minutes, media analysis coverage reports, research notes and proposals. Make sure that you follow the guidelines, sometimes set out in templates, so that your outputs are consistent and follow the same style rules.

As a rule of thumb, it is sometimes worth considering that less is more. Most of us in a professional environment are swamped with writing we have to digest – if yours can be succinct and cut to the chase, it will be welcomed more than most. As with every other aspect of the written word in PR, make sure that you use a spell checker to ensure your copy does not contain silly errors which will undercut what you are actually saying.

Common client outputs include:
– Monthly progress reports
– Media coverage summaries
– Meeting Minutes
– Research notes
– Proposals
– Recommendations

Technical and specialist

Depending on your role as a PR professional there are certain job roles or client accounts on which you may be asked to display a high degree of technical or specialist knowledge. An example of this might be in the field of investor relations, where you are working for a client company which is a quoted stock and which is dealing in communicating some highly complex financial information to analysts in the City.

You may not know some of the technical terms or indeed the language which is used in this context, so it is advisable to make sure that you do not commit to something that you cannot realistically deliver. The PR profession has specialists who have come from other careers and who understand a wide range of complex and sometimes arcane issues which need to be communicated in writing. Where this is the case, it is up to you to recognise what you can or cannot realistically deliver.

There are a range of specialist or technical outputs which, however, you may well be asked to process in the course of your job. These could include specialist reports, market research and PR surveys and articles which you may be required to ghostwrite for your clients. In all these cases it is best to take advice from colleagues and managers before committing to produce copy which you cannot process without the requisite knowledge.

Technical & specialist outputs:
- Research reports
- Surveys
- Technical articles
- Analyses

Technical process & importance of accuracy

Credibility and reputation generally depend on public information being substantiated and accurate. In the corporate communications and PR profession, the integrity of information you manage is therefore paramount. As with journalism, going public with information that is factually incorrect has the capacity to damage reputation, prompt crises and even provoke legal action, such as *libel or slander.*

It is built into the professional codes of practice that PR professionals must be truthful and must ensure their work serves the public interest over and above the interests of any single client. But part of being a PR professional is understanding the power of the written word to influence opinion and change behaviours, and thus the packaging of information to show a product or service in its most favourable light is a skill set you need to develop. However, facts need to be accurate and opinion verifiable.

It is your responsibility to ensure that information distributed meets the highest standards. *Approval mechanisms* are generally in place with a client or in your own organisation to prevent any unauthorised or unchecked information being distributed to media or other audiences without being signed off by all relevant parties. In some cases, for example, with information that relates to a company's stock price, a news release might even have to be sent through the legal department for additional sign-off.

Fact checking

In British journalism, *double sourcing* is the rule which states that a fact is not true until it has been verified by two independent sources. This is time consuming and often difficult to effect, but it acknowledges a central point which is that the facts we often take as given do not always constitute the truth. Part of your role in managing the written word through the PR process is to make sure that facts are checked and opinion substantiated before information goes public. Any organisation consistently sending out information that is incorrect and inaccurate is putting its reputation at risk.

When going public with information, most especially in a media context, there are some basic rules of engagement which determine how that information can be used. It is worth knowing and remembering these, for example when giving information to journalists in a briefing note or interview. (See Chapter Eight: Media interviews & presentations).

Editing & sub-editing

In public relations, use of the written word divides into two distinct parts. Content is about what you say and delivery is about how you say it. Delivery, or packaging, of the content is critical as it needs to follow certain rules if it is to conform to *best practice*. In other words, without mastering the packaging of copy into recognisable outputs, you cannot really be regarded as professional or even effective.

The art of assembling and presenting PR copy is, in essence, journalistic. Much of the craft skills of journalism, including editing, sub-editing, proof reading and caption writing are core skills for any jobbing journalist and have transferred into PR to shape the common written PR outputs, such as news releases, features, marketing copy, reports, briefing documents and positioning statements.

Editing

An editor is the person who assembles copy from different sources and puts it together to form a cohesive whole. Editors tend to have the big picture and take a lead role in deciding on what stories, features, pictures and promotions will be included in a house magazine or newsletter (or newspaper if they are a journalist). As an editor, you may also commission written contributions on subjects that are topical or you want readers to know about. Editing skills mean writing editorial opinion pieces (op-eds), *drafting briefs* for writers to respond to, *setting word counts* so that people write to length and deciding on which pictures, charts, graphics or clips to use to create an overall design and feel for a publication.

Sub-editing

Sub-editing is a skill which emanates from newspaper journalism. It aggregates all the skills required to produce copy that conforms to the required style. Thus it will include cutting copy so that it fits a word count; it will include writing headlines and subheads, setting sentence and paragraph lengths and making sure that terminology, grammar and punctuation are perfect. Proofreading is the final part of the process that ensures copy is ready to print or sign off.

PR professionals are required to use both editing and sub-editing skills in the course of the job, and it is here that the house style guide, which sets out the way in which copy is presented, is most helpful as it provides a framework that can be quite quickly learned and applied.

Individual elements of the sub-editor's job would include ensuring copy conforms to house style in the following ways:

Headings and titles

The reader sees the heading first. A heading should be short but explain what text will come after it. Headings and subheadings generally have a capital letter for the first word only, for example:

'How to make money by working from home'
In writing news, headlines should have a subject, object and active verb:
'Man bites dog'

Subheadings

Subheadings help direct people to the right section of the page and to break the page down into more manageable chunks. Capital letters are generally used for the first word only, applying the same rules as for headings.

Paragraphs

Keep paragraphs short and have one blank line between each. In news releases and features, paragraphs should not usually be over two sentences (between 35 and 50 words).

Bold

We avoid using bold in text. It can be distracting. However, if you need to *emphasise* text, use bold rather than italics or block capitals, as it is easier to read than the other two.

Italics

You should avoid using italics as much as possible. Do not use italics for online copy as they are even more difficult to read on screen.

Jargon

You cannot assume that people reading your copy understand the jargon used in specialist or technical subjects. Don't use scientific words or foreign phrases, unless they are widely accepted, if a common word is available. Sometimes you can use jargon if the text is aimed at a specific audience who are familiar with it.

Abbreviations and acronyms

When you write abbreviations (where a word is made shorter by leaving out some of the letters, or by using only the first letters of each word) or acronyms (a series of letters which stand for the name of an organisation and can be pronounced as though they were a word), do not use full stops between the letters. Here are some examples.

- FCO (Foreign and Commonwealth Office)
- RAF (Royal Air Force)
- NHS (National Health Service)

When you use abbreviations or acronyms, you must first write them out in full with the abbreviation or acronym afterwards:

House of Commons (HOC)

Chief Executive Officer (CEO)

Job titles

Where there is a choice use lower case for job titles. Capitals are only generally used in 'Chief Executive Officer' or 'Chairman'.

Numbers

Numbers from one to nine are written as words. Numbers of 10 upwards are written as figures.

Use of grammar

Grammar is a big subject and one that is often widely misunderstood or poorly applied. However, grammar, punctuation and spelling dictate the final quality of a written output. Poor grammar detracts from the credibility of a piece of writing, reflecting on the author but also on the organisation itself.

If you are distributing information publicly it is important to check that you have followed the most common grammatical rules alongside the organisation and style of the copy. Again, a style guide should help you stay on track.

It is useful here to flag up some of the most common errors and pitfalls in the way in which grammar is used.

The reflexive pronoun

We have been advised to write to yourselves regarding the incident at the town hall last week.

Any problems, please contact myself on the number below.

It will be myself who will be handling your account.

Myself, yourself, herself are reflexive pronouns – they reflect back to the personal pronoun.

For example:

I'm going to have to do it myself.

You only have yourself to blame.

We have been advised to write to *you* regarding …

Any problems, please contact *me* on the number below.

You do not want to write copy with ambiguous meaning, but look for clarity of meaning and expression:

Ambiguity

If it looks nice in the morning, I'll take my bike to work.

As the most fuel-efficient Ford in the range, you benefit from lower fuel and road tax costs.

Clarity

If the weather is nice in the morning, I'll take my bike to work.

As the most fuel-efficient Ford in the range, the Focus benefits you with lower fuel and road tax costs.

Tenses

Make sure that the tenses you use are consistent. If something is happening in the present, use the present tense, don't mix it with past tense as it presents a time sequence that is confusing.

GRAMMAR QUIZ

Work out what is wrong in the following phrases. You will find the answers at the back in Chapter Thirteen.

1. "We are taking the advise of the Emergency Services" said Bill Bloggs "and closing the factory immediately".
2. Its always myself whose doing the cooking.
3. Neither Sara or Vicky are going to the beach.
4. Thank you for inviting David and I to give our presentation.
5. Now that the weather is better there's far less black clouds in the sky.

---

6. As the leading authority on alternative energy our wind technology is the most efficient alternative to fossil fuels.
7. Gemmas taking a fortnights holiday because she can't bare Vanessas kids in the office.
8. The product has some unique USP's.
9. Having had a chance to review the proposal, giving the time available, deciding not to pursue newdevelopment.
10. North Western Health Authority has, today announced plans to open a second Special Cancer Unit, at the North Western City Hospital, in Sheffield.

Spelling, punctuation & proofreading

In the UK we use British rather than American spelling. For example, 'organisation' rather than 'organization'. Many PC based spellcheckers are US versions, so you need to be mindful of this when proofreading copy for spelling errors.

As a rule of thumb, all PR copy needs to be *proofread* before being sent to a client or journalist, so a good idea is always to get a colleague to check your copy for grammar, punctuation and spelling to ensure there are no mistakes.

You should use punctuation that is grammatically correct and use only as much as you need to make your meaning clear. Do not double up punctuation. For example, do not put a dash after a colon or a colon after a question mark.

There are varying rules for punctuation depending on house style, but as a general rule, the following guide represents a broad consensus on punctuation.

Full stops
Leave two blank spaces after a full stop.
Do not use a comma if a full stop and a new sentence would be more appropriate.
Do not use full stops after abbreviations (BA, Mr)

Comma
A comma adds a pause in a sentence and you can use commas to break up items in a list. You do not need to put a comma before 'and' in a list.

Colon (:)

Use colons to start a list if the bullet points form complete sentences only when they are read with the introductory sentence.

Quotation marks
Use a colon before quotes, and put quotation marks around the speech or writing you are quoting.

Clive said: "I can't seem to understand the basics of grammar."

Bullet points (lists)
Bullet points or lists provide a simple and effective way of getting messages across. They usually follow a heading or an introduction which ends in a colon or a full stop.

If the introduction is not a full sentence (that is, the words after the bullet points form a sentence only when they are read with the introduction):

- end the introduction with a colon (:);
- don't use a capital letter at the beginning of each bullet point, unless it is the name of a person or organisation;
- use a semi-colon at the end of each point;
- keep the grammatical structure the same for each point in the list;
- make sure each point is a similar length (shorter is more effective);
- use 'and' or 'or' after the end of the second-last bullet point of your list; and
- finish the last point with a full stop.

Dashes
Dashes are different from hyphens. They are a different length and are used for different purposes. Dashes may have spaces on both sides, depending on how you are using them. When we use numbers always use 'to'.

People aged 45 to 55

Commonly an unspaced dash is used to link two items which are equally important, where the dash replaces the word 'and'. For example:

The Jones – Smith marriage

Dashes can be used to separate a clause in a sentence – like this – and give a clearer, longer break than commas.

Apostrophes
When used correctly, apostrophes indicate possession (something belonging to someone or something) and in some cases abbreviation (to show a word has

been shortened). The apostrophe goes after the person (or thing) that owns whatever the word describes. So if the word is singular the apostrophe goes before the 's', and if the word is plural the apostrophe goes after it (except for words which are already plural, such as 'children' – in this case, the apostrophe goes before the 's' – 'children's).

Examples:

The boy's toys (one boy), boys' toys (more than one boy).

Family's house, families' houses, residents' association, children's home, managers' seminar.

People often get confused with 'its' and 'it's', which are often written incorrectly. 'Its' is the possessive form of 'it', like 'your' is the possessive form of 'you' and is a complete word in its own right. 'It's' is short for 'it is' and the apostrophe shows that the second 'i' is missing.

An easy way to remember this is that if you can replace 'his' or 'hers' with 'its' then there's no apostrophe. You don't need to put apostrophes in abbreviations such as MPs, unless you are showing possession, as in 'the MP's surgery'.

Etc.

The use of 'etc.' is mostly lazy. Use 'and so on' instead of 'etc.'. However, it is best to say what you mean and not leave it to the reader to decide what we mean by 'and so on'.

Exclamation marks

These have no place in well-written text unless – and this is very rare – you want to express surprise, shock or anger.

Wow!

You surprise me!

You should only use one exclamation mark at once.

Hyphens

Hyphens make words easier to read, for example:

- co-operate
- co-ordinator
- by-election

As words become commonly used, they tend to lose their hyphen. The following should not have a hyphen, and should be written as one word.

- website

- email
- helpdesk
- fundraising
- antisocial

Proofreading

Proofreading is the process whereby you check your copy for accuracy, grammar, punctuation and spelling and ensure that it conforms to house style. All copy needs to be proofread before it is distributed internally or externally. It is your responsibility to ensure that all your copy is error free. Normally, there will be a system of approvals in place through which a manager or client must 'sign off' a piece of copy to formally approve it and authorize its release. Make sure you know what this approvals process is and follow it at all times.

Proofreading is a journalistic and publishing skill which deploys a system of marks which indicate to a printer where changes need to be made to copy on a printer's proof or galley. Although these formal marks are not used very often in PR, it is very useful to know what they are.

WRITING EXERCISE:

See if you can proofread the following pieces of copy. Be aware of grammar, punctuation and spelling. Use a spell checker to make sure you don't let any spelling mistakes slip under the radar. Check your answers against those at the back of the book in Chapter Thirteen.

Copy 1:

A Breathe Of Fresh Air

Were holding a free event on air polution and offering a limited No. of free smarter driving sessions. Air polution can have: a negative affect on your health, and your environment. To find out more about its impact, whats being done to takle it and how to protect yourself, come along to our Air Quality Summit. Its on Mon 21/11 from 5.00 to 8.30pm at Chiswick Town Hall, on Power Road. Whats more we have a limited No. of free, 1 hr smarter driving training sessions on offer. You must hold a full driving license to take part. Simple smarter driving tecniques can save you around 15 per cent on fuel. To book yr place for either of these activities email airquality@chiswick.gov.uk or call the number below.

www.chiswick.gov.uk/airqualitysummit

Telephone:

Copy 2:

Drummond park Care Home

Work has begun on the new Drummond Park Care Home.The sixty bedroom residential and nursing care home with thirty-five extra care shelterd flats will offer greater space and comfort helping residents to remain independant for longer. Care Staff will also be available day and night. There will also be Guest Rooms, a Café and an Exercise Room in bright, attractive buildings, together with landscaped gardens.The Home is due to open in early 2013

chiswick.gov.uk/homesforolderpeople

CHAPTER ELEVEN

The Caterpillar Life

The PR consultancy market; the talent pool; education & CPD; specialists vs generalists; agency hierarchies; job descriptors; a life in the day.

The PR consultancy market

The PR profession in the UK is growing all the time. Whilst the industry rate of growth might have slowed down since the credit crunch in 2008, it is still estimated to be worth a total of £7.5 billion. Most PR agencies increased their fee income by 10% or more in 2011 and the top 150 UK consultancies alone account for some £900 million of fee income between them.[*]

Whilst it is hard to access definitive figures, this UK industry growth is echoed globally. For example, the PR consultancy industry in the United States was estimated to be worth an annual $3.4 billion in 2010.[**] Evidence is also provided by the massive expansion in the footprint of the global PR brands in the Middle East, Far East, Asia and Latin America. Over and above geographical expansion of the majors, there has been further growth in the numbers of home grown agencies in emerging markets, encouraged by deregulation and democratisation, the increase in the bandwidth of communications channels, especially social media, and the increasing sophistication of consumers.

The International Communications Consultancy Organisation (www.iccopr.com) now represents 1,500 agencies around the world via their membership of trade associations in 28 countries. Consumer communications, aided by increasing attention to social media and some regulatory changes from government in Washington, are helping to grow the consultancy industry in the

[*]PR Week: Top 150 Consultancies Report 2011
[**]Communications Industry Forecast, Veronis Suhler Stevenson

United States by an average annual rate of 11%, according to the ICCO World Report 2011. The consultancy industry in Brazil grew by 23%, in Russia by 17% and by a comparable percentage in India in the same period, according to the report.

Industry sectors which have been identified as growth areas for future business for PR consultancies include energy, healthcare and the financial sector. In many countries, with the exceptions of those where large-scale cuts are already underway, the public sector also provides the promise of future work. On the downside, the retail, automotive and real estate sectors appear to hold out the least promise in the short term.

The talent pool

To support this growth trajectory requires a steady supply of both recruits to the industry and the retention of staff already employed. Evidence suggests that staffing represents the single biggest challenge to the continuing success of the PR industry. In its 2011 report, ICCO says that the issue of attracting talent and then retaining it 'proves to be of major concern to PR consultancies. Growing the business depends on achieving the right mix of skills and experience and having the ability to form lasting relationships with clients'.

Like most industries, PR is governed by the law of supply and demand. However, in a people based business, it is relatively more important to have a pool of qualified, talented and motivated individuals to fulfil the agency promise, deliver a high quality service and provide innovation and service development in line with, or ahead of, the demand curve.

Education and CPD

One measure of the maturity of the PR industry over the last 30 years is the growth in academic options for those wanting to either enter the profession or develop the knowledge and skills to go further when they are already part of it. For example, there has been a proliferation of Bachelor of Arts (BA) degrees in the UK which offer public relations as a major study option, some of them including meaningful job placements. Institutions offering choices here include the University of Central Lancashire, The University of Lincoln and the University of Greenwich. Masters degrees (MAs) are on offer from providers such as Bournemouth University, De Montfort, Leeds Metropolitan and the University of Ulster. A wealth of qualifications can also be gained from independent providers offering face-to-face and online options.

A more recent development, over the last decade, is the development of Continuing Professional Development (CPD) programmes for those PR professionals who are Accredited Practitioners in membership of the Chartered Institute of Public Relations. Part of the obligation of Chartered status is to ensure that practising professionals keep themselves up to date with developments by setting aside a fixed number of hours every year to dedicate to increasing their knowledge and skills base.

Specialists vs generalists

For those graduates or school leavers contemplating a career as a public relations consultant, there is a wide and growing choice of options. The global PR brands, companies like Hill & Knowlton, Burson-Marsteller and Edelmans now span the world, having built a geographical footprint which encompasses the mature western markets in which they have a well established presence, alongside emerging markets such as Brazil, Russia, India and China, and frontier markets including those in some Middle eastern countries, Africa and Latin America.

The US PR consulting firm Burson-Marsteller, for example, has grown into perhaps the largest and best known PR consulting firm in the world today, with nearly 70 wholly owned offices and 71 affiliate offices in 98 countries across six continents. With its strong internal culture of training and developing its people into fully rounded professionals, the business makes a virtue of offering candidates a wide choice in both practice area and geographical location.

Within these firms, it is possible to both generalise and specialise, as the function of scale means the client base spans B2B, consumer, public sector and third (charity) sectors, as well as all the niche practices you can find, for example: public affairs; corporate social responsibility (CSR); financial and analyst relations; crisis planning and management; media relations; and digital communications, including social media. Working within the corporate envelope of one of the industry majors brings opportunity and challenge, but amongst other things it will mean learning and adapting to a proprietory consulting methodology, with its accompanying view of the world. Comprehensive in-house learning, training and mentoring programmes make this option attractive for many graduates and others seeking a clear career path.

Alongside the industry majors, however, there is a further raft of medium sized to large companies based in the UK from which to choose. The Public Relations Consultants Association (PRCA) alone represents nearly 250 consultancies, along with 60 in-house departments. Within these, it is possible to select individual operators which offer vertical sector specialisation in healthcare, real estate, energy, investor relations, fashion and so on.

The best advice is to match your own specialisms and ambitions as closely as possible with the appropriate providers. In its annual breakdown of the PR consultancy industry, *PR Week* even isolates lists of the top consultancies in each niche area, for example the top 50 digital, consumer or technology consultancies, so identification of a niche operator is often quite straightforward.

The PR consultancy business, though, mirrors the wider UK business landscape in the sense that most of its companies are small, or even micro businesses, often with a sole owner and one or two employees. These small firms are often set up and launched on the basis of the reputation and experience of the founder, perhaps an in-house PR & communications director or manager with a network of contacts and a successful track record in a specific industry sector who has decided to go it alone. In these organisations, whilst one can gain a holistic, end-to-end experience of the PR business, there is no clear career progression and the employee is also open to any eccentricities, as opposed to orthodoxies, of the owner manager.

It is a common pattern that is reproduced, with it perhaps being worthwhile to note that the PR profession is highly entrepreneurial and often attracts those with a particular personal vision, method, energy and commitment. There are perhaps two other significant factors: first, it is not necessary, though it is desirable, to be formally qualified as a public relations practitioner in order to set up a business; whilst the industry is moving towards standardising, examining and qualifying the profession in order to regularise it, in fact anyone could still start up in business as a PR consultant; and second, the entry costs are very low, really only requiring a desk, a laptop, broadband connection and mobile phone to be up and running. This makes it a very egalitarian and meritocratic profession, based almost entirely on intellectual rather than physical assets.

There is a debate in the profession, as with some others, as to whether good PRs are born or made. One school of thought suggests that certain skills can be taught, but that others are inherent. The alternative school, based perhaps on a more process driven ideology, believes that anything can be taught, it is a matter simply of mastering the required skills and then applying them via direct exposure and experience. There is of course no objective solution to this debate, only a series of personal views formed through observation and experience.

Agency hierarchies

Consultancies or agencies are most often still organised in a traditionally hierarchical fashion, with the most senior – and expensive – people at the top and the most junior – and cheapest – at the bottom. This makes sense for obvious reasons, because the model accommodates both a management and fee structure that makes both organisational and economic sense (see Chapter Two: The PR Consultancy Business Model). However, the hierarchical or top-down model is not the only possibility.

There are a now a number of consultancies which are organised around a *flat structure*, which has the effect of raising the fee threshold at the bottom of the organisation, knocking out layers of management in the middle and creating more of a recognisable partnership model, where the organisation coalesces around an administrative 'core' which fuels the interests of the individual partners (much like, say, a barristers' chambers). There are others, though not many, that are organised in an entirely different way, around skills sets such planning, management, client handling and creativity, more along the lines of an advertising agency.

The traditional PR consultancy hierarchy, though, would be organised firstly into divisions or 'practices', so that the business is fundamentally structured in a way that makes sense of its specialisms, for example in public affairs, consumer, B2B or professional services. Beyond that, it would have a structure that both accommodates the nature of the work, usually defined by the creation of 'accounts' alongside the responsibility for management, which is devolved as the organisation moves away from the top management layer. So the 'pyramidal' structure of a typical medium sized consultancy might look like Figure 1 opposite:

Job descriptors

It is, by definition, hard to be categorical about what the job of PR consultant requires at any given point. The nature of the job, at the heart of a premium service industry, means that it can generate a wide variety of demands at any

Figure 1: TYPICAL CONSULTANCY HIERARCHY

Company Principal				

Director	Director			

Account Director	Acct Dir			

Acct Manager	Acct Mngr	Acct Mngr	Acct Mngr	

Account Executive	Acct Exec	Acct Exec	Acct Exec	Acct Exec

Account assistant	Acct asst	Acct asst	Acct asst	Acct asst	Acct asst

given moment, some of them highly unpredictable. It is this variety and unpredictability which offers some of the allure; a job which is never the same on two consecutive days can be highly prized by those who are by nature flexible, adaptable and opportunistic. At the same time, this spontaneity and inability to predict the precise flow of work, is the very reason that some entrants find the role too random and therefore ultimately untenable.

So what would the typical consultant be asked to do at different levels of the hierarchy? Is it possible to be prescriptive about some aspects of the job function? I believe that it is possible to draw some basic distinctions in the characteristics of the role, covered by general headings, between the varying levels outlined in Figure One, as follows:

Company Principal
- Company leadership
- Strategic and business planning
- Financial management

- Sales and marketing plan
- Client relationships
- Talent management, incentivisation
- Quality control
- Performance

Board Director
- Divisional leadership
- Revenue stream and financial targets
- Client relationships
- Delivery of agency promise
- Quality control and results
- Team leadership and management

Account Director
- Responsibility for client portfolio
- Revenue stream and new business targets
- Team building and management
- Client liaison
- Delivery of outputs and results
- Monthly account deliverables
- Monitoring of time
- New business inputs

Account Manager
- Management of client portfolio
- Team management
- Time management
- Delivery of outputs
- Achievement of results
- Weekly client liaison
- Workstream planning
- New business inputs

Account Executive
- Daily client liaison
- Weekly programme delivery

- Press Office management
- Story identification
- Forward features programmes
- Planning and management of events
- Social media management
- Speaker programmes
- Evaluation and activity reports
- Time management

Account assistant
- Desk research and analysis
- Media monitoring
- Social media monitoring
- Reports
- Timesheets
- Meeting minutes
- Account administration
- Client liaison
- Distribution of outputs

A life in the day

It is of course helpful to put some general headings in the boxes above; taken together, they provide an overview of what the end-to-end PR consultancy job looks and feels like. But how do these headings translate to something more grounded in everyday reality? Here I have included just a few fictional portraits of the daily realities of some of these roles.

Jenni C: Account Executive, Excellent PR

Jenni has been working at Excellent for a year, and has been in PR consultancy for three years. She is currently working on four separate accounts, two of which are major high street consumer brands. Jenni is also working on the launch of an online retailer as well as a new account in the travel and tourism sector. In any given week, Jenni is mainly focused on media and blogger relations, constantly looking for story and photo ideas from which she can develop news releases and story pitches for her primary target journalists on the national dailies and consumer magazines. Jenni is also closely monitoring the activity on Facebook pages that have been set up for the accounts, together with organising some special promotions and photo shoots on new product offers. She is supervising the monitoring and evaluation of media coverage and other results, such as online traffic, blogs and tweets which contain client product mentions. Over and above this, Jenni has been asked to attend a brainstorm the agency is organising as part of its new business pitch for a famous high street designer who is looking to launch a fashion line in the Autumn. Jenni has to compile her weekly activity reports and also must remember to fill in her time sheets on the desktop project management system before Friday.

Bob D. Account Director, Banzai! PR

Bob is in his mid-thirties. He has been in the PR business for a decade and came into the business via an initial career in market research. A graduate in economics and statistics, Bob was attracted to the creativity and flair demanded by public relations consultancy, tied to the opportunity to leverage further his knowledge of markets, business trends and statistics. Bob is responsible for managing a team of six people, including two account managers and two account executives. Between them they are managing seven retainer based clients, bringing in a substantial six-figure revenue stream to the agency. Bob is doing high-end analysis of the trends and issues impacting his clients' business and is in constant touch with senior managers on the client side. He is overseeing the delivery of the agreed programmes of PR activity, checking monthly reports with his account managers and monitoring results and quality. He is also fixed on generating some new business opportunities to reel in to the group and is always working on proposals and pitches which might help him to meet his new business targets. Bob is also involved in doing appraisals for his team and is currently dealing with some issues relating to one junior staff member who is seen to not be performing. Bob grapples with handling his own twitter stream but is doing his best.

Alison B. Account assistant, Robin Hood PR

Alison graduated last year from Bournemouth University with a BA degree in PR and communications and this is her first job. Over three years, and with a work placement in between, she has built up a good grasp of the principal theoretical underpinnings of the modern practice of public relations. Whilst she has mastered the principles of the profession, she is only now getting to grips with the nuts and bolts of a typical PR programme and what it means in terms of inputs, outputs and consequent responsibilities. As an account assistant, she has work coming at her from all directions and initially found it difficult to manage her time. She is compiling media and blogger lists, updating online press offices with current information and doing phone ring rounds to check that agency managed events will be attended by invitees. She is also helping with research on venues and costs for a roadshow which the team is planning for a client. Alison is compiling weekly and monthly activity reports and passing them across to the team; she is also dealing with inbound client enquiries and fielding them to the appropriate executive. It is also her job to monitor and collate media coverage and build it into reports, so she is liaising with two different media monitoring companies. Last week, Alison attended her first brainstorm, which she really enjoyed, and made a contribution which she was proud of.

CHAPTER TWELVE

Caterpillars of Wisdom

Introduction; P.T. Barnum, the greatest showman of them all; Ivy Lee, founder of modern PR campaigning ; Edward Bernays, the engineer of consent; Carl Byoir, surviving the un-American Activities Committee; Harold Burson, taking public relations to the next level.

Introduction

Whilst public relations is still a young profession, no more than a century or so into its trajectory, it has already started to build a formidable body of knowledge which now forms the theoretical and educational base underpinning the modern practice of PR. This advance into the academic hemisphere is an inevitable step in the legitimisation and codification of the profession and a necessary step for the educative process.

PR students now have access to this body of knowledge through literature, video, case studies and personal accounts. There can be no excuse, as a public relations practitioner, for not assimilating the lessons of others and assessing models and examples of applied PR which have been tried and tested in the marketplace.

There is a much less overt footprint though, of the individuals who were the pioneers of the PR profession, those who navigated uncharted waters to adapt an infant discipline tested in the centrally funded public arena to the more profit oriented and goal focused private sector. Not only did these pioneers, men like Ivy Lee and Edward Bernays, have the nerve and entrepreneurial skill to set up in business, but they had to do it in such a way as to convince clients of their value with neither a professional body behind them nor the weight of precedent. One measure alone of their achievement is that an entire industry has been built on their shoulders, one which shows every sign of establishing a global footprint as it moves into the spaces opening up between other, less accommodative and versatile marketing and promotional disciplines.

The achievements of these first practitioners are all the more formidable when you take into account that their client base rapidly spread to include rich and powerful individuals alongside some of America's greatest corporations and even embraced foreign governments intent on harnessing the new science of persuasive communications to further their national interests. In this process, we almost universally find big risk takers prepared to back their judgement and sometimes, in the case of Carl Byoir, for example, to risk their own resources in order to reel in the first long-term retainer client. With the distance of history, we find that some of the decisions made by these pioneers were variable in their moral distinctions, but we never see a loss of self-confidence or ability to innovate and push the boundaries.

Above all, it is perhaps the figure of Edward Bernays who must take most credit for establishing a body of theory founded in science to underpin the applied nature of his work. A nephew twice over of the great Sigmund Freud, Bernays was precociously clever and able to translate his brilliance into a series of written works that between them chart the legitimisation of the new field of public relations 'counsel'. These works, *Propaganda* and the *Engineering of Consent* being perhaps the best known among them, are widely read and referenced today by academics and commentators wishing to chart the growth trajectory of public relations and its growing headspace in the public mind.

These brief thumbnail sketches of five of the great pioneers and innovators of public relations are designed to give a glimpse into the world as it was up to and after the First World War, showing the origins of the profession and its subsequent journey across the 20th century into the 21st, as the analogue age gradually gave way to the digital revolution.

P.T. Barnum: the greatest showman of them all

"Let's get the show on the road."

Phineas Taylor (P.T.) Barnum, born in Bethel, Connecticut in 1810, has been referred to as the patron saint of promoters. He is a man greatly mythologised and someone who in his time took promotion and the business of publicity to new heights. Whilst he talked things up and was a shameless self-promoter (in many respects he could be said to have actually invented the notion of advance publicity), he was also a great action man and doer, a polymath with parallel careers as a writer, politician and entrepreneur marking him out as a high achiever.

Like all truly memorable individuals who accomplished remarkable things, he was a big risk taker. Barnum's life was never plain sailing and his middle years especially were to be dogged by failure, litigation, debt and public humiliation before he secured his reputation and made a fortune along the way.

Photos of P.T. Barnum reveal a substantial man in conservative suit and bow tie, with receding hair, a firm jaw and a robust physique, often posed from the recesses of a high backed chair. His gaze seems direct and full of self-confidence, as indeed it should have been. An entrepreneur in his early 20s, Barnum founded a weekly newspaper before moving into an 'entertainment career', or what we might reasonably think of as showbiz.

Barnum's entry point to this more fragile means of livelihood was via his purchase of Scudder's American Museum, which he renamed modestly after himself. The museum became a showcase for grotesques and human curiosities, including General 'Tom Thumb'. However, his most audacious move came in 1850, when he promoted the US tour of singer Jenny Lind, allegedly paying her $1,000 a night for 150 nights.

Barnum's place in history, though, was forged by his founding of the Barnum & Bailey Circus, a ground-breaking and substantial enterprise which became its own legend and which he promoted as 'the greatest show on earth'. With its grandiose and high-profile tours across the major cities of the United States, the circus became a household name, carving a domestic and international reputation. With no television, and little or no popular cinema at that time, the circus became a byword for excitement, innovation and flair.

It was in the promotion and advance publicity for these tours that Barnum truly found his metier. He had a genius for influencing the public mood through a series of stunts, photo opportunities, special appearances and provocative stories which he seeded in the press.

The examples of Barnum's imaginative approach to bringing in the bucks for his shows are manifold, and it is sometimes hard to know whether some of these accounts are apocryphal.

For example, Barnum hooked up an elephant to a plough and put this formidable combination to work on the fields of his property in New York. Given that the property fronted onto a commuter railway line, the press were soon knocking down his door to report the story. "Newspaper reporters came from far and near and wrote glowing accounts of the elephantine performances," he wrote.

Another account sees Barnum hiring an orchestra to play at the entrance to his museum, an initiative which he promoted using the strapline: 'Free music for the millions'. The trick was that he picked an orchestra that was so bad, the crowds attracted by the free offer soon took refuge by paying to get into the musem and away from the cacophony outside. "I took pains to select and maintain the poorest band I could find, one whose discordant notes would drive the crowd into the museum, out of earshot of my orchestra," he said.

Perhaps the most imaginative story of all recounts the tale of a man who entered Barnum's office at his museum one day looking for work. At a minimal wage, Barnum enlisted the man to take a few loose bricks to the corner of the building and put them down. Thereafter, at regular intervals, he continuously exchanged the bricks for new ones. A large crowd of onlookers soon gathered to witness the 'brick man' and many of them would accompany him into the museum, entry for which they of course had to pay. Barnum is said to have taken particular pride in this stunt, which he claimed contained all the pure elements of his promotional philosophy: "It employed novelty, demonstrated ingenuity and achieved free publicity," he noted.

A true American original, P. T. Barnum coined a number of phrases which have since passed into the everyday lexicon, among them: 'let's get the show on the road'; and 'throw your hat in the ring'.

The first universally acknowledged user of striking advertisements, stunts and stories to promote his product, Barnum above all recognised the value of working with the press. "There was only one liquid a man could use in excessive quantities without being swallowed up by it, and that was printers' ink," he wrote.

Ivy Ledbetter Lee: founder of modern PR campaigning

"Tell the truth, because sooner or later the public will find out anyway."

Just a glance at the public relations career of Ivy Ledbetter Lee reveals a string of firsts, pulled off by a man who is still rightly considered a pioneer of the practice of modern public relations.

For example, it is Lee, a graduate in economics from Princeton University and former journalist on the *New York Times*, who is credited with writing the first ever press release, which he did after the 1906 Atlantic City train wreck, convincing the Pennyslvania Railroad Company to disclose information to journalists before they got the facts from somewhere else; not only that, but he also invited reporters and photographers to the scene of the accident, going so far as to organise a special train to get them there. This act alone has led some to regard Lee as the father of modern crisis relations.

With his friend George Parker, he founded one of the earliest public relations firms, Parker and Lee in 1905, and thereafter the much longer lived and better known public relations counselling office, Ivy Lee & Associates, in 1919. His press releases were greeted by newspapers with some hostility; they were seen as thinly disguised advertisements and blatant tools of manipulation. This response helped propel Lee to issue his *Declaration of Principles*, which articulated for the first time the public responsibilities that PR practitioners have beyond their immediate obligations to their clients.

This *Declaration* was sent to all newspapers to clarify Lee's position and build bridges. It began: 'This is not a secret press bureau. All our work is done in the open. We aim to supply news. This is not an advertising agency. If you think any of our matter ought properly to go to your business office, do not use it ... in brief, our plan is frankly, and openly, on behalf of business concerns and public institutions, to supply the press and public of the United States prompt and accurate information concerning subjects which it is of value and interest to the public to know about.' The *Declaration* went on to make major points about factual accuracy, general discretion and the importance of newspaper reporting at the expense of newspaper advertising.

A well connected and highly networked man, both professionally and through his marriage to Cornelia Bigelow, Lee held down some of the highest profile and most senior PR positions in American life, serving as publicity director of the American Red Cross in World War One and representative of the Rockefeller family and its Colorado Fuel and Iron Company, which had been savaged in the press for its strike breaking, anti-union reputation after the massacre of miners in Ludlow, Colorado in 1914.

As personal PR counsel to John D Rockefeller, Lee is credited with turning around the public's image of him and his company. He enabled the public to get a glimpse into his boss's life for the first time through film of him playing golf and giving away dimes to children.

Lee is also credited as being largely responsible for enabling the development of public relations departments and teams within large corporations. His work as an adviser and counsel to corporates, amongst them the manufacturing giant Bethlehem Steel, showed the way for future generations of PR and communications professionals. Whilst at Bethlehem Steel, he is said to have advised managers to list their top priorities and work on tasks in that order, a suggestion for which the Bethlehem Steel CEO Charles Schwab paid him $25,000. Lee's other corporate clients included General Mills and Lucky Strike; he was PR counsel to individuals including Charles Lindbergh and Walter Chrysler, amongst others.

However, like all pioneers and ground breakers, Lee's career was not without controversy. Like Barnum before him, he took risks and became the victim of some of his own poor decision making.

In what we now might see as a leap of the imagination, Lee's separate career moves laid him open to charges of sympathising with and promoting the interests of both the Nazi Party in Germany, and the Russian Communist Party. Despite his professed commitment to two-way communications, he was more widely accused of being a propagandist on behalf of clients generally despised by the public. Shortly before his death, US Congress began investigating his work in Nazi Germany on behalf of the company I G Farben, manufacturer of, amongst other products, equipment that was used in concentration and extermination camps. He also came under the spotlight for doing his bit to try and improve US and Soviet trade relations by openly representing the Soviet Union, perhaps in retrospect not the most popular role he ever performed.

Despite these inevitable question marks, Lee's legacy and achievements are considerable. He indisputably played a major role in shaping the parameters of the modern practice of public relations, moving it into the centre of corporate life and elevating the role and status of public relations counsel to an entirely new level. In both media relations and crisis relations, he was instrumental in defining the practice and laying the groundwork for future relationships between corporations and the public.

He is single-handedly credited with helping the American Red Cross become the major recipient of funding from the US public during World War One. Lee was also an inaugural member of the Council on Foreign Relations in the US when it was established in New York City in 1921.

One piece of advice said to have been dispensed by Lee to the heir to the Standard Oil fortune has echoed down the years: "Tell the truth, because sooner or later the public will find out anyway. And if the public doesn't like what you are doing, change your politics and bring them into line with what people want."

Edward Bernays: the engineer of consent

"If you can influence the leaders, either with or without their conscious co-operation, you automatically influence the group they sway."

In his autobiography, '*Biography of an Idea*', Edward Bernays recounts how a famous foreign correspondent of the Hearst newspaper empire, Karl Weigand, came to dinner with him at his home in 1933. During dinner, Weigand talked about the Nazi information minister, Josef Goebbels, and his propaganda plans to consolidate Nazi power.

"Goebbels had shown Weigand his propaganda library, the best Weigand had ever seen. Goebbels, said Weigand, was using my book '*Crystallising Public Opinion*' as a basis for his destructive campaign against the Jews in Germany. This shocked me ... obviously the attack on the Jews of Germany was no emotional outburst of the Nazis, but a deliberate, planned campaign," he wrote.

Crystallising Public Opinion was written in 1923. The book was to be followed by many others, among them *Propaganda*, written in 1928 and *The Engineering of Consent*, first written as an essay in 1947. These and other influential works positioned Bernays unequivocally as the leading theorist, thinker and philosopher of modern public relations. Whilst some of his theory has been disputed and even discredited, his work has unquestionably shaped the profession, and indeed certain aspects of modern life, more than any other individual. So much so, that Bernays was named one of the top 100 most influential Americans by *Life Magazine*.

In *The Engineering of Consent*, Bernays coined the term to define the art of manipulating people, who he saw as fundamentally irrational and unable to be trusted. Furthermore, he suggested that entire populations were undisciplined and lacking in intellectual or definite moral principles; this in turn left them vulnerable and thus susceptible to wanting things that they didn't really need. This was achieved by linking products and ideas to their unconscious desires. In short, through the manipulation of unconscious desires, consumer psychologists could make choices for people before they bought a product, without those people even being aware they were being manipulated.

In applying this principle, one of Bernays' favourite techniques was the indirect use of 'third-party authorities' to plead for his clients' causes. When he was hired to promote bacon, for example, he commissioned a survey of doctors and reported their recommendation that people should eat a hearty breakfast. The results of the survey, along with publicity promoting bacon and eggs as a hearty breakfast, were sent across the US to 5,000 doctors.

It is alleged that the marriage of bacon and eggs and its subsequent adoption as perhaps the classic breakfast stemmed from this one act. More importantly, though, in this one example we see that Edward Bernays can take responsibility for the concept of third-party endorsement, arguably the single most important principle underpinning the practice of modern public relations.

Bernays had first become struck by the effects of propaganda and its wider possibilities when he had attended the Paris Peace Conference in 1919 as a member of the US Committee on Public Information (CPI). He had been working for the administration of Woodrow Wilson during the First World War, promoting the idea that America's war effort was bringing democracy to all of Europe.

The wholesale acceptance of this democracy message by the public led him to consider whether the wartime propaganda model could be taken and used in peacetime. He knew though, that the negative associations with the word 'propaganda', due to its use by the Germans, made its continued use unacceptable. He therefore came up with the alternative 'public relations counsel', a term which he was to use to describe himself when he set up in business in a small office in New York City in 1919. An account of this thought process is provided by Bernays himself, in an interview he gave for the camera and which is included in the classic 2002 BBC television series 'Century of the Self', made by Adam Curtis.

Origins of theory

Throughout his long life (he died at the age of 104), Bernays was not shy of making a great play on his close relationship with his uncle, Sigmund Freud. Born in Vienna in 1891, Bernays was in fact a double nephew of the pioneer of modern psychoanalysis, both through blood and marriage. Whilst his family moved to New York a year later, in 1892, Bernays grew up to develop a view of the world that was to be closely influenced and shaped by the theories of his famous uncle.

Bernays drew heavily from Sigmund Freud's exploration of the power of the unconscious mind to drive human behaviours. He also drew on the work of Walter Lipmann, whose *'Public Opinion'* was published in 1922, Wilfred Trotter, a British surgeon who wrote *'Instincts of the Herd in Peace and War'* and the French writer Gustave Le Bon, the originator of crowd psychology. It was Bernays who could himself be said to have pioneered the PR industry's adoption of psychology and other social sciences to design its public persuasion campaigns.

Bernays was careful to draw a major distinction between the new discipline of public relations and the older established business of advertising, seeing advertising men as 'special pleaders', paid only to persuade people to accept an idea or commodity, whereas he characterised the PR counsel as a creator of events that dramatised new concepts and perceptions, and which in turn influenced leaders and societal groups. "Of course, you know, we don't deal in images, we deal in reality," he told the American academic and writer Stuart Ewen on a visit to his home in 1990, when Ewen presented Bernays with a gift of his own book, 'All Consuming Images'.

Some of the principal contradictions in Bernays' theories, more visible with time, coalesce around his views about democracy and its central role in public relations. Whilst he championed the role of PR in a democratic society, he was something of a paternalist if not a despot in his general view of people as reactive and less intelligent than the elite who he believed should control and dictate to the many.

Bernays unashamedly saw himself as part of that elite and to some extent had little respect for the average person's ability to think out, understand or act upon the world in which they were living. He told Ewen that the PR professional aims his craft at a general public which is essentially, and unreflectively, reactive. Working behind the scenes and out of view, the PR expert is an applied social scientist, one educated to employ an understanding of 'sociology, psychology, social psychology and economics' in order to influence and direct public attitudes. In 'This Business of Propaganda' he wrote, however, that the lure of a retainer or the demands of a client should not subvert the public relations counsel from their wider duty to society as a whole.

Torches of Freedom

In addition to his use of third-party endorsement, Bernays believed in 'interrupting' the normal course of events to create news, and he was extremely successful, using news releases, photo-opportunities and stunts to draw attention to his clients and their products. For Lucky Strike, one of his major corporate clients, Bernays organised perhaps his best known PR campaign of all, to promote cigarette smoking in public amongst American women, a major taboo in the 1920s. He did this by orchestrating a stunt during the 1929 Easter

Parade in New York City, getting a group of models to simultaneously light up Lucky Strikes and declare them to be 'Torches Of Freedom'. He had alerted photographers to the fact that this was going to happen and they were there to record the event in dramatic pictures. Following this, more American women began smoking in public, a habit which gradually became socially acceptable, and which was largely attributed to Bernays.

Alongside relentless self-promotion, Bernays turned his brilliant mind to the promotion of cars, fashion, soap and books. His client list includes some of the best known American corporate names, among them Proctor & Gamble, the American Tobacco Company, Cartier, CBS, the United Fruit Company and Dodge Motors. He was credited with inventing the tie-in, a process via which one occasion for promoting a consumer product is linked to another, for example using media relations, events and advertising in an integrated way, creating a powerful and influential promotional wave. He also worked, like his contemporary Ivy Lee, for government departments, charities and even countries. In the 1950s his ideas and vision contributed towards India being portrayed as the most democratic country in Asia, through his part in persuading the government to adopt a Bill of Rights.

But it is perhaps for the rigour and enduring power of his philosophy and writing which between them helped shape the 20th century discipline of public relations that he is best remembered. Despite the cracks that have opened up in his reputation since he espoused his views, the body of work – both theoretical and applied – make him a giant of the profession and one whose influence and impact spread to every layer of the consumer society that we recognise today. "In almost every act of our daily lives, whether in the sphere of politics or business, in our social conduct or ethical thinking, we are dominated by the relatively small number of persons who understand the mental processes and social patterns of the masses. It is they who pull the wires which control the public mind," he wrote in 1928, in his book *Propaganda*. Public relations has travelled a great distance since then, but his words continue to be just as prescient.

Carl Byoir: Surviving the Un-American Activities Committee

"No citizens will be burned at the stake in this country by irresponsible attacks, even in high places."

When the public relations counsel Carl Byoir made this declaration, he was speaking after a debilitating and potentially catastrophic investigation by the Federal Bureau of Investigation (FBI) into the possibility that he had been engaged in un-American activities. On trial in July 1940, he had been accused by US Congressman Wright Patman of alleged Nazi propaganda activities. The attack was seen by Byoir as a thinly disguised attempt to discredit him and thus his opposition to the congressman's chain store tax bill, a bill that he had opposed in his capacity as public relations counsel to the Great Atlantic & Pacific Tea Company.

At the depth of the Great Depression, governments had been looking for ways in which to conjure up new sources of revenue, much as they are doing again across the western world. A movement to tax chain stores emerged, one which directly threatened A & P's business and about which the owners said: "If the people of the United States like our stores so little that they are willing to tax us out of business, that is their affair. We will shut up our shop."

In a news release recording the clearing of Byoir's name, issued by the Jewish Telegraph Agency on 17th July 1940, Byoir was quoted as saying: "I know that the public is not interested in an individual case, but I feel there is an important principle involved here. It would be a terrible situation if, in times of great public feeling, citizens had no protection against malicious accusations attacking their loyalty made on the floor of Congress by a congressman abusing his legal immunity. Many people do not know that under this immunity a congressman cannot be sued for slander for anything he says in Congress."

How had Patman felt it possible to make such an accusation? In 1933, Carl Byoir & Associates, then a growing and successful PR consultancy, began working on a tourist travel promotion for the German Tourist Information Office. According to published sources★, the client George Sylvester Viereck asked for the firm's assistance in increasing tourism to Germany, beginning a $108,000 contract with the German Tourist Information Office. The firm went on to accept a $4,000 cash advance from the German Consul General in New York for distributing press releases to improve Germany's image in the United States, in response to publicity about German anti-semitism.

The work undertaken by Carl Byoir & Associates on this account was the source of Patman's accusation in 1940 and of other earlier problems between 1934 and 1935. Byoir, though, was no stranger to controversy. Only three years previously, in 1930, he had done a deal with President Gerardo Machado of Cuba to invest his own money in a promotional drive to market Cuba as a premier holiday spot.

In 1930, Byoir had leased two newspapers in Havana, the *Havana Post* and the *Havana Telegram*. Wanting to boost circulation, but not attracted by a conventional marketing solution, he decided to increase the numbers of American tourists visiting Cuba.

In a deal he struck with Machado, Carl Byoir was to invest his own capital to increase tourism and, in return, receive a five-year contract worth $300,000 to hire his new company as the public relations office for the Cuban government. The arrangement was highly successful, leading to an increase from 80,000 tourists to 165,000 in a single year. Machado was the firm's first client and the relationship proved highly controversial in years to come.

A newspaper editor at 17

Carl Byoir, born to Polish Jewish immigrants, started his working life in newspapers. At the age of 17, when his editor at the *Waterloo (Iowa) Times* was struck dead by a heart attack, Byoir stepped into his shoes. His early career was many layered but always showed a remarkable capacity for making money. In 1911, he bought the franchise for the Montessori school system, travelling to Italy to learn how the system worked from the founder, Maria Montessori. Byoir went on to build up an immense amount of experience and success in newspaper advertising, working for the Hearst magazine empire, and in the process revolutionising the advertising approach and revenue of *Cosmopolitan* magazine.

It was in 1917, though, that he found himself alongside Edward Bernays working for the US Government on its Committee on Public Information (CPI). His relationship with Bernays was both a personal and professional one, and the two went on to start up a business together, Byoir first enlisting the support of Bernays in promoting the effort of Lithuania to get itself recognised by the US Senate. In his memoirs, Byoir wrote: "After the war, Eddie and I started a little publicity business, and believe me it was a little business. It was so little, that I decided to go into something more profitable."

Over the ensuing years, Byoir built his business into a formidable public relations consultancy, working for a wealth of major corporate names, including Crosley Motors, Easter Railroads, Freeport Sulphur Company and the Great Atlantic & Pacific Tea Company. He also worked for the Franklin D Roosevelt administration planning many charity balls for the President and helping to

*The Museum of Public Relations (www.prmuseum.com)

establish the March of Dimes Foundation.

Byoir died in 1957, but his company prospered for some time after that, before it was finally taken over by Hill & Knowlton. The contribution he made to the profession is marked by his continued presence in published accounts of its history and development.

Harold Burson: Taking public relations consulting to the next level

"PR is no longer a corporate step-child. CEOs increasingly realise the value of public relations."

Harold Burson, one of the joint founders of the global public relations consultancy Burson-Marsteller, was described in a survey by *PR Week* at the end of the 1990s as 'the century's most influential PR figure.' This view, though it might be disputed by some purists, needs to be taken seriously. Burson, along with advertising man Bill Marsteller, founded the company in 1953 and it has grown into perhaps the largest and best known PR consulting firm in the world today, with nearly 70 wholly owned offices and 71 affiliate offices in 98 countries across six continents.

Burson himself, though he stepped down as CEO in 1988 and is now in his 90s, still checks in for work, writes a blog, gets out and about to speak at industry events and is self-confessedly enthused by circulating with young people in the profession. One of the characteristics that marks him out in the business is his commitment to placing training and development at the top of the agenda, believing both in attracting top candidates into the PR profession and keeping them there by developing them as rounded practitioners rather than simply specialists operating in silos. He observes that, across his professional life, the most accomplished PR practitioners have been those he calls 'Renaissance people'. "We are not striving hard enough to attract the brightest and the best into careers in public relations," he says.

Burson has equally strong views about the purpose that public relations is set up to serve, believing that too many modern definitions miss the point that part of the job is to see that clients are serving the public interest alongside their own, with a focus needed on client vulnerabilities as much as strengths, and an ability to be "intuitive about the gremlins around the corner along with the demons today."

In his own words, Burson posits that public relations is a process that impacts public opinion, with the objective of motivating individuals or groups to take a specific action. This can be done, he says, in only three ways: seeking to change a presently-held opinion or attitude; seeking to create a new opinion or attitude; and reinforcing an existing opinion. "That's why we write and try to place articles and stories where they will be read or heard; that's why we think up outrageous stunts certain to attract media attention," he says.

If he is known for a particular skill within the field it is in the high-octane specialism of crisis relations and he has acted for many high profile corporate names battling with reputation-threatening nightmares. One client, Johnson & Johnson, found itself in September 1982 having to withdraw a product, Tylenol, from the shelves completely following the deaths of several customers who had taken capsules found to be laced by an intruder with cyanide. Burson's advice to the company on managing its way through the crisis helped lead to the development of tamper-proof packaging and has gone on to be classed in the industry as the 'gold standard' in this particular area.

Much as it was praised for its level of strategic advice and tactical acumen on behalf of Johnson & Johnson, the company received wide criticism for its acceptance of a brief from US firm Union Carbide following the 1984 disaster at its Bhopal plant in India, when a gas leak killed over 2,000 people. Consultants from Burson-Marsteller were brought in to organise communications following the leak and provide advice to Union Carbide executives, one of whom – CEO Warren Anderson – ended up being temporarily placed in custody in an Indian jail when he appeared on the scene having followed advice from his legal and PR team. Burson himself, according to published sources, was always proud of his company's work in helping the media cover the story.

Like most major players in the world of PR consulting, Burson and his company have taken risks and courted controversy in some of the choices made over the years. Neither implementing communications programmes for the Argentinian military dictatorship in 1976 nor the Indonesian government after a massacre in East Timor in 1991 endeared the company to the human rights lobby. Most recently, the company's bungled attempt on behalf of Facebook to seed negative stories about the privacy policies of Google has caused it to lose some credibility according to published sources.

From his vantage point at the very summit of the profession, Burson has views he is not slow to express on many of the major tides and currents that ebb and flow around the practice of public relations, among them the impact of the Internet, the growth of numbers of women in the profession and reasons behind the failure of PR to take its seat at the Boardroom table alongside more mature and better paid disciplines such as the law and management consultancy. He also believes that too little is known amongst today's practitioners about the founding fathers of the profession and their enduring influence upon it.

"PR is in my view a two-stage process. The first stage is embarking on a pattern of behaviour; the second stage is effectively communicating to target audiences the message that persuades audiences to specific courses of action. Nowadays, too many messages are in the interest of the communicator, rather than in the interests of the public," he says.

CHAPTER THIRTEEN

Test Yourself!

Chapter Two Exercises: The PR consultancy business model

In this exercise, both calculators are required in order to estimate the time needed to deliver certain outputs alongside the time needed to manage the account. In the estimate below, I have calculated, for example, that the email management briefing would take roughly the same time as that required to research and draft a feature.

EXERCISE 1: The Group Safer Drivers campaign: Deliverables

ITEM	AD	AM	AE	Admin	Cost
Email management briefing	Feature				£810
Article for the Flagship	Feature				£810
Web page dedicated to Brake	Feature				£810
Media relations: *motoring trade and consumer press*	Two news releases				£700
Media relations: *Websites/womens' editors regionals/nationals*	Two news releases				£700
Media relations: *Young drivers – consumer mags/radio stations*	Two news releases				£700

ITEM	AD	AM	AE	Admin	Cost
Briefing for journalists and report presentation	1 day	2 days	3 days	3 days	£3,090
Press Office x 3 months					£5,280
Account management and client meetings(x8)	2 days	4 days	4 days		£4,720

EXERCISE 2: Group Factors Campaign
Team and Programme budgets and fee breakdown

1. The Budget:
£70,000 for 12 month campaign
Fee: £60,000: expenses: £10,000; print & production: (outside budget)

2. The Team
- Principal/Director: Overall quality role; client advocate
- Account Director: Team Leader, monthly direction/control
- Acct Mgr/SAE: Day to day client contact/implementer
- Account Executive: Implementer
- Admin: Backup.

3. Programme Outputs
3.1. Admin and Management Tasks
Monthly client meeting: half day AD; half day AM; day AE (x12)
Six monthly review meetings: half day CP; half day AD (x2)
Press cutting collation & analysis (press office)
Press distribution lists (press office)

3.2. Deliverables
Press office function (12 months x £1,760.00 pcm)   21,120.00

Press pack   1,454.00

Two news releases per month (£350 per release)   8,400.00

Write three booklets:
(3 days AE, two days AM per booklet: 1,840)   5,520.00

Write four newsletters, plus two inserts:
(4 days AE, 2 days admin, 2 days AM per newsletter: (2,420)   9,680.00

Concept & draft for one survey (half day AD, day AM. Day AE)1,180.00
Identify & brief strategic partners (one day AD, two days AM)   1,800.00

                                                              49,154.00

Group Factors Account: Fee breakdown

Hours	CP	AD	AM	AE	Ad
Press office	0	42	84	168	168
Press pack	0	1	7	21	0
News releases	0	0	24	168	0
Newsletters	0	0	56	112	56
Booklets	0	0	42	63	0
Survey	0	3.5	7	7	0
Partner briefing	0	7	14	0	0
Monthly meeting	0	42	42	42	0
6 monthly review	7	7	0	0	0
TOTAL HOURS	7	102.5	276	581	224
P/MNTH	0	8.5	23	48	18
P/MNTH CHARGE	0	969	1633	1920	378
MONTHLY RETAINER:	**£4, 900**				

Chapter Three Exercise: New business development

EXERCISE 1: Set out a proposition and supporting USPs for 'My PR Firm':

Proposition:

My PR firm turns your communications spend into business capital
USP 1: We give you measurable return on investment when you commit to us

USP 2: We understand your issues because we move in your world
USP 3: We can show you five ways of using communications to improve on your bottom line

Chapter Four Exercise: Winning PR proposals

EXERCISE: interrogate a PR brief, Dept of Health Flu Awareness.

1. Pick up the phone and call three national and specialist healthcare journalists. Find out if they are aware of the campaign and the target to reach vulnerable groups. Find out how they like to get their information, check whether they would be interested in attending a face-to-face press briefing. Download the subsequent intelligence into your proposal.
2. Make a couple of calls to special interest groups to find out how they might respond to forging an alliance to spread the message about the free vaccine. For example, Help The Aged, might be prepared to enter into a strategic partnership to disseminate information and create a response mechanism for pensioners wishing to get immunised. This would make a major splash in your proposal.
3. Try and make contact with one or two community leaders of hard-to-reach groups, such as Somalis or Bengalis in London and find out how they recommend opening up lines of communication with community members. Do they want printed information in own language or word of mouth, and how do they like to engage with healthcare issues? Would women be able to visit a doctor's surgery if necessary?
4. See if you could identify and make contact with one or two champions or potential ambassadors across the target audience groups. Perhaps a call to their agents, if they have one, or direct if you can reach them. Would they be prepared to put their name to the campaign and, if so, would they do it for free or would it involve a charge? If so, how much?
5. Call up the editors of three or four ethnic newspapers or radio stations. Ask them how they would be prepared to engage with the campaign and what kind of press information they would require, and in which languages. Would they be prepared to come to a press briefing or do an interview with a campaign spokesman? If so, what kind of criteria would they be working with?

NEWS WRITING EXERCISES

Release One:
Audience: Consumers
Media target: national newspapers
Sample correspondent: Home affairs correspondent, *The Times*
Angle: Helping the fight against crime in inner city areas

NEW CITY SUPERCOPS USE JETPAKS TO HELP BEAT CRIME

London, (date). A new generation of flying policemen, using space programme rocket technology, may soon be patrolling the skies of inner-city Britain. Today the US based Jetpak Corporation launched a campaign to sell up to 250 new 'Mercury' Jetpaks to regional emergency services across the country and is optimistic it will reach its targets.

Mercury is a jet propelled backpack which a policeman or fireman can use as a highly manoeuvrable, rapid response vehicle to reach accident or crime victims. It has applications across the fire, ambulance and police services.

The aim is to cut violent crime and make neighbourhood streets safer to walk in, as well as speeding up response times for fire and ambulance staff. Home Office crime statistics show violent crime in inner cities is on the increase, up by 4% on the year. The company has already received a license from the Home Office for its invention.

"With Jetpak, we can speed up current response times in a range of life threatening situations blighting hard-to-reach reach inner-city locations," said Jetpak CEO Dan Carruthers.

News release Two: specialist
Audience: Procurement departments, emergency services
Media target: Vertical sector press
Sample correspondent: Editor, *Police Review*
Angle: This equipment will help meet rapid response targets

JETPAK OFFERS EMERGENCY SERVICES HIGH TECH ROUTE TO SPEEDIER RESPONSE TIMES

London, (date). Now the emergency services can access a new, space-age weapon in the fight against inner city crime and boost rapid-response times in life-threatening fires or accidents. The Mercury Jetpak, developed by the US Jetpak Corporation, goes on sale today to emergency services across the country.

It is being offered as a potent new weapon in the fight to keep inner city crime under control, and to meet more demanding response targets across all three emergency services. Emergency services response times are currently failing to meet targets by an average of 8%, with the ambulance service performing worst of all, according to recent statistics.

The Mercury is a lightweight pack powered by rocket fuel and strapped onto the back of the user. It employs jet propulsion and finger controlled navigation systems to manouevre in tight situations.

"This is a major step forward in the ability of all the emergency services to get to an incident very rapidly. In hard to reach inner city areas especially, it could well be a life-saver," said former Chief Constable, Perry Mason.

At £150,000 per unit, the Mercury will not be cheap, about the same price as a new, fully equipped ambulance. However, it has already received the backing of some of the top law enforcement, health and fire chiefs in the country.

News release Three: High Net Worth Individuals (HNWI)
Audience: High Net Worth Individuals (HNWI)
Media Target: HNWI Media
Sample correspondent: News editor, *How To Spend It*
Angle: Exclusive travel accessory

MERCURY JETPAK BEATS THE RUSH HOUR BLUES

London, (date). Now the smart commuter with a spare £150,000 can have the ultimate executive travel accessory.

A new and simple backpack on the market from today enables users to fly to work, out to lunch, or even off on an out of town weekend.

Developed by US firm, Jetpak Corporation, the Mercury can only be bought by those prepared to take a demanding flying exam and lessons to master the back-up procedures required to keep refuelled and ready for flight, as well as pay the asking price.

The company is stressing that the vehicle, due to be in use with the emergency services across the country this year, is much more than an executive toy.

"Mercury has important uses in the rapid response field, but there is no reason why private individuals cannot take advantage of its amazing speed and manoeuvrability, especially in inner urban settings where traffic flows can be inhibiting," said Jetpak CEO, Dan Carruthers.

Chapter seven exercises: wider and deeper with features

FEATURE EXERCISE 1: Milestone feature for supermarket magazine

THE SWEET TASTE OF CHOCOLATE BOOSTS XMAS PULLING POWER

Have you ever wondered about the secret to Casanova's success, and what exactly it was that turned him into such a legendary lover?

Well the answer may be closer than you think. In fact, you might just be a wrapper away from the recipe for passion power right now.

The fact is that Casanova was reputed to drink chocolate, rich in cocoa, every night before he hit the sack. For the legendary lothario, his nightly hit of choccie was just the stimulant he needed to get in the mood.

Could the chocolate have been Chocmaster's? No. Should it have been? You bet. Over £160 million worth of Chocmaster chocolate will be sold this Christmas, proving that it is right up there with music as the food of love.

Chocolate is recognised as an age old aphrodisiac. Chocaholic Gail Simmons even calls it a drug.

"When I eat good quality chocolate, I feel a sense of well-being flood through me. But is has to have a high cocoa butter content," she raves.

The British chocolate industry is worth over £3.5 billion a year and the average Briton packs away 16kgs per annum.

And the secret formula behind its success? Its all down to a sneaky little substance called Phenylethylamine.

This, science tells us, is the chemical substance in chocolate that appears to confirm the 'sex substitute' theory of chocolate consumption.

And women are especially susceptible.

That can only mean one thing. For a seriously loved up Christmas, girls, get chomping on choccies.

After all, it is better to end up with a winning recipe than a complete turkey.

FEATURE EXERCISE 2: News feature for consumer/business magazine

NEW WASHING POWDERS FAIL TO GET THE GREEN LIGHT

First the good news. As of this week, you can buy three 'green' washing powders which are designed to help you do your bit for the environment.

Now the bad news. No one can seem to agree on whether they actually do what they say they do.

So are they really green? Or are they all hot air and bubbles?

Friends of the Earth spokesman, Tony Hype is in no doubt that there is something fishy in the laundry basket.

"It is impossible to say from the labeling on these products whether they are environmentally friendly or not," he states. "Guidelines on packaging must be strengthened if consumers are able to become informed purchasers of environmentally safe products."

The fact is that all of these new products have their upsides and downsides.

But none of the manufacturers is prepared to bite the bullet and dump their existing winners.

One example of this is I N Store, marketing manager for BRAND Z. "We can't just withdraw all our old products because customers are very attached to them. Besides, we're not saying they're bad, just that this is better," he explains.

Sound like hedging to you? It does to us.

There are other worrying signs that the wheels may be coming off the green washing powder wagon before it really gets rolling.

"Too expensive," says one housewife we door stepped at a London supermarket this week. "I'll try them but I can't help wondering if I am being conned," says another.

However, we are not being prescriptive about any of Brand X, Y or Z. You should check them out, where you can find them.

But we do ask ourselves; has the green washing powder bubble burst already? Ends.

CHAPTER NINE EXERCISES: The PR launch

EXERCISE 1: the PR launch of Minipets

The pre-launch campaign kicked off with a sneak preview of MiniPets to a handful of opinion-forming journalists who were invited to a private room at the ToyFair trade show in the Spring.

To tap into the Japanese technological reputation, the PR team organised a live web-cast from the Japanese Toyfair in May. A Japanese presenter was used to give the product 'authenticity' and street-cred. Over 300 media were sent a mailer to invite them to logon to see the launch.

A series of one-to-one media previews were given in Japanese themed locations including Nobu and Yo!Sushi to build interest prior to launch and secure major editorial features.

A 'miniature' mailer inside the toy's packaging was sent to all relevant youth, gadget and national media but no product. In order to get their hands on a MiniPet, media had to contact the press office, enabling them to create a database of 'MiniPets mates'.

Finally, the toys were unveiled to over 200 journalists at a July press conference.

Launch and Build

All relevant media received a MiniPet on the day of the launch.

From July onwards, releases/photography were fed to the media which capitalised on topical stories. These included:

- **July** – MiniPets playing on a Subuteo football pitch to tie in with the World Cup
- **August** – Release based on Japanese miniature trends including micro-scooters
- **September** – MiniPets on a sushi plate in Yo!Sushi
- **October** – A MiniPet in the mouth of a Japanese Sumo wrestler
- **November** – The Race of the MiniPets – pitting characters against character
- **December** – Announcing a shortage of MiniPets and emergency new shipments

AA Ltd approached The Guinness Book of Records to persuade them to agree a world record for the smallest interactive toy. This was exploited as an opportunity for a December photo call (results: *The Sun* and *Daily Star*) and an additional news story.

Working closely with Hamley's and an independent toy seller in Bournemouth, they leaked the 'news' that MiniPets was the best selling toy for Christmas. This was accompanied by a photo call with cute children with their pets and a quote from toy retailers talking about the demand for the product.

The on-going PR campaign helped to encourage The British Association for Toy Retailers to choose MiniPets as one of The Top 10 Toys, further guaranteeing MiniPets a place on Christmas present lists. On announcement day, AA Ltd ensured that every relevant TV programme had a set to demonstrate.

TV programmes included *CITV, RI:SE, Richard & Judy, The Saturday Show and Milkshake* were all targeted in the months before Christmas to maintain a TV presence up until the big day.

Evaluation and measurement

Within a month of the Summer launch, MiniPets had become a best selling toy, helped by widespread publicity that then continued to grow in the run-up to Christmas.

MiniPets achieved blanket national coverage (appearing at least once in every daily national newspaper including *The Financial Times*) over the course of the nine-month campaign. Media coverage also encompassed many weekend newspapers and supplements, more than 200 regional newspapers, over 70 radio stations, 30 children's titles, 20 websites.

The toys were shown on 14 television programmes including *ITN* and *Sky News*. The combined audience exceeded 95 million. There were also 9 features in the toy trade press to maintain interest from retailers in MiniPets.

MiniPets' sales success is the ultimate testament to a strong PR campaign. Sales were reported of one million units in at a retail value of £10 million.

Chapter Ten Exercises: Writing style

EXERCISE 1: Grammar Quiz

1. "We are taking the advice of the emergency services and closing the factory immediately," said Bill Bloggs.

2. **It is** always **me who is** doing the cooking.
3. Neither Sara **n**or Vicky **is** going to the beach.
4. Thank you for inviting David and **me** to give our presentation.
5. Now that the weather is better, **there are** far **fewer** black clouds in the sky.
6. As the leading authority on alternative energy, **we are confident that** our wind technology is the most efficient alternative to fossil fuels.
7. Gemma**'s** taking a fortnight**'s** holiday because she can't **bear** Vanessa**'s** kids in the office.
8. The product has some **USPs.**
9. Having had a chance to review the proposal, **and** given the time available, **we have decided** not to pursue **the** new development.
10. North Western Health Authority **has today** announced plans to open a second Special Cancer **Unit at** the North Western City **Hospital in** Sheffield.

EXERCISE 2: Sub-editing test

Copy One:

A breath of fresh air
We're holding a free event on air pollution and offering a limited number of free smarter driving sessions. Air pollution can have a negative effect on your health and your environment. To find out more about its impact, what is being done to tackle it and how to protect yourself, come along to our air quality summit. It's on Monday 21 November from 5 to 8.30pm at Chiswick Town Hall on Power Road. What's more, we have a limited number of free, one hour smarter driving training sessions on offer. You must hold a full driving licence to take part. Simple smarter driving techniques can save you around 15% on fuel. To book your place for either of these activities email airquality@chiswick.gov.uk or call the number below.
chiswick.gov.uk/airqualitysummit
Telephone:

Copy Two:

Drummond Park Care Home
Work has begun on the new Drummond Park Care Home. The 60-bedroom residential and nursing care home – with 35 extra care sheltered flats – will offer

greater space and comfort, helping residents to remain independent for longer. Care staff will also be available day and night. There will also be guest rooms, a café and an exercise room in bright, attractive buildings, together with landscaped gardens. The home is due to open in early 2013.

chiswick.gov.uk/homesforolderpeople

Telephone:

CHAPTER FOURTEEN

Glossary and Terms

Financial Jargon Buster

In the course of learning how to manage money and other financial considerations, there may be occasions when those who know more than you about the subject try and blind you with science by using words or concepts you do not have a grasp of. Don't let them win that easily! Get a grip on some of the terms that you will need to compete on an equal footing. Look at some of these for starters.

Activity based costing (ABC): This is a more complete way to understand what drives costs as it allocates each cost in proportion to several business features, such as office space.

Assets: Generally, anything in a business that has some sort of financial value and can be converted to cash.

External Audit: The annual, statutory process via which chartered accountants formally assess a company's financial performance for tax purposes in order for records to be submitted to Companies House.

Balance Sheet: Snapshot of the financial health of an organisation at a particular point in time.

Capital budgets: Expenditure on large capital items such as premises, IT systems, equipment or machinery.

Cash flow statement: A record of the movement of cash in and out of the company, designed to be predictive as well as historical.

Debt-To-Equity ratio: A measure of the extent to which a company is financed by outside creditors versus shareholders and owners.

Depreciation: Represents the loss of value of a fixed asset and is a method of allocating the cost of the asset over its useful lifetime.

Double-declining balance: This method of depreciation is known as an accelerated method of depreciation because it pushes the majority of the total depreciation amount into the early years of ownership.

Double-entry bookkeeeping: The formula which states that every transaction on one side of the accounting equation results in a transaction on the other side. This observation – the basis of the entire science of accounting – was made in 1494 by Luca Pacioli, an Italian mathematician and Franciscan monk.

Management accounting: The systems that allows you to track financial performance, usually monthly, against budget.

Operating profit/loss: The positive or negative balance left after all fixed and variable costs have been deducted from a trading statement.

Profit Centre: A department or team which is expected to produce a revenue stream and profit for the business as a whole, and which is accounted for separately by senior management.

Rechargeables: Sometimes known as third-party costs, or bought-in costs, these are items which you buy on behalf of clients and charge them on, usually with the addition of a handling fee.

Return on Investment (ROI): The measure by which investors, usually shareholders, calculate what their money has earned for them over the course of an accounting year. For a shareholder, ROI would be in the form of a dividend.

Spreadsheet: The software format, such as Excel, which displays figures in rows and columns and enables formulae to be programmed in order to make automatic calculations affecting the figures.

Timesheets: Either a manual or a computerised method for recording and analysing time spent against activity. Fundamental to managing any professional or consultancy based business.

Trading Forecast: Another term used to describe a budget, meaning an annual projection of a company's performance expressed in figures.

The accounting equation: The foundation of the science of accounting, this equation states: Assets = Liabilities + Owner's Equity

Top-down budgeting: The term applied to the budgeting system which simply restates the year before within a variance of plus or minus 10%.

Variable costs: Expenditure which is not committed every month and thus provides the option to cut or reduce if required.

Variance: The accounting term used to describe the difference between budgeted and actual income or expenditure.

Zero based budgeting: Sometimes known as bottom up budgeting, this questions the relationship between costs and benefits. It means you have to justify all expenditure from the ground up, stating its specific purpose and outcome.

Sources for The Caterpillar Factory

★ *Managing Budgets*, Stephen Brookson, Dorling Kindersley, part of the Essential Managers series, 2000.

★ *Personal Networking*, Mick Cope, FT Prentice Hall, 2002.

★ *The Complete MBA For Dummies*, Dr Kathleen Allen, USC Business School and Peter Economy, author of Managing For Dummies, Wiley Publishing, Inc, 2007.

★ *Surviving and Prospering in the Small Firm Sector*, Graham Hall, Manchester Business School, Routledge, 1995.

★ Chartered Institute of Public Relations, Cream Awards Case Studies.

★ *Selling To Win*, Richard Denny, Kogan Page, 2001.

Print Journalism: A Critical Introduction, Richard Keeble, Routledge, 2005.

Observer Style Guide: http://observer.guardian.co.uk/styleguide.

The Public Relations Handbook, Alison Theaker, Routledge, 2001.

Public Relations Strategies & Tactics, D.L. Wilcox, G.T. Cameron, Pearson International Edition, 2007.

★ *Flat Earth News*, Nick Davies, Chatto & Windus, 2008.

★ *The Facebook Effect, the Inside Story of the company that is connecting the world*, David Kirkpatrick, Virgin Books, 2010.

★ Paul Holmes: the Holmes Report, 2012-07-09 www.holmesreport.com

★ *Right Side Up, Building Brands in the Age of the Organized Consumer*, Alan Mitchell, Harper Collins Business, 2001.

Managing Public Relations, James E Grunig, Todd T Hunt, Harcourt Canada 1984: Characteristics of the four models of public relations.

Mediadisk (www.mediadiskonline.com).

Response Source (www.responsesource.co.uk).

Gorkana (www.gorkana.com).

The Art and Craft of Feature Writing, William Blundell, New American Library, 1988.

ICCO World Report: A Return To Growth (www.iccopr.com).

Century of the Self, Adam Curtis, BBC, 2002.

PR! A Social History of Spin, Stuart Ewen, Basic Books, 1996.

Propaganda, Edward L Bernays, H. Liverlight, 1928.

Harold Burson, www.haroldburson.com

The PR Museum, www.prmuseum.com

INDEX